Designs for *Primitive* Rug Hookers

By Jenny Rupp and Lisa Yeago

We would like to thank our families for their love and patience with this addiction we call rug hooking. They have supported us through piles of wool, smells from the dye kitchen, and trips to camps and shows. We also want to thank Alice Strebel and Sally Korte for their advice, encouragement, and friendship. It is priceless.

TABLE OF Contents

FROM THE *Editor*

Primitive and wide-cut rug hooking is enjoying unprecedented growth in the fiber arts world. Perhaps it's the time element involved—primitive projects can be completed quicker than fine-cut projects—or maybe it's a fascination with the history of our past.

Hooked rugs, considered to be America's one indigenous folk art, first appeared in the eighteenth century in Atlantic Canada and New England. At that time, rug hooking was considered to be a craft of poverty. Our predecessors used any materials they had on hand—old clothing, blankets, feed sacks—to create rugs to cover their bare floors. Most designs were uncomplicated and primitive—proportion and perspective often were disregarded. These charming rugs of yesteryear still have appeal today and reflect life in a simpler time.

Whatever the circumstances that draw you to the primitive look—whether you are a beginning or experienced rug hooker—hooking and completing a small project is appealing. Accomplishing a finished piece of work such as a purse, pillow, or tablemat is fun to do and provides an immediate feeling of accomplishment. Today's rug hookers have gone beyond making strictly utilitarian floor coverings to also making small projects such as wallhangings, purses, mats, tea cozies, and more.

Well-known primitive rug hookers Jenny Rupp and Lisa Yeago combine their expertise along with the talents of 19 others to bring an exciting variety of hand-hooked projects. Now, with the introduction of *Designs for Primitive Rug Hookers*, these easy-to-follow projects become clear for the novice as well as the most experienced rug hooker. Each article contains a materials list, hooking and finishing instructions, a pattern line drawing, designer's tips, and contact information about the artist.

For a good look at what rug hookers are doing with yesteryear's craft, pick up a copy of *Rug Hooking* magazine, or visit our web site at www.rughookingonline.com. Within the world of rug hooking, and *Rug Hooking* magazine, you'll find a style to suit every taste and a growing community of giving, gracious fiber artists who will welcome you to their gatherings.
—*Ginny Stimmel*

Designs for Primitive Rug Hookers

EDITOR
Virginia P. Stimmel

ASSISTANT EDITOR
Lisa McMullen

BOOK DESIGNER
CW Design Solutions, Inc.

PHOTOGRAPHER
Impact Xpozures

CHAIRMAN
M. David Detweiler

OPERATIONS MANAGER
Anne Lodge-Smith

Presented by
R·U·G HOOKING

5067 Ritter Road
Mechanicsburg, PA 17055
(717) 796-0411
(800) 732-3669
www.rughookingonline.com
rughook@stackpolebooks.com

PRINTED IN CHINA

ISBN: 1-881982-55-6;
978-1-881982-55-5

Canadian GST #R137954772.

WHAT IS *Rug Hooking*

Some strips of wool. A simple tool. A bit of burlap. How ingenious were the women and men of ages past to see how such humble household items could make such beautiful rugs?

Although some form of traditional rug hooking has existed for centuries, this fiber craft became a fiber art only in the last 150 years. The fundamental steps have remained the same: A pattern is drawn onto a foundation, such as burlap or linen. A zigzag line of stitches is sewn along the foundation's edges to keep them from fraying as the rug is worked. The foundation is then stretched onto a frame, and fabric strips or yarn, which may have been dyed by hand, are pulled through it with an implement that resembles a crochet hook inserted into a wooden handle. The compacted loops of wool remain in place without knots or stitching. The completed rug may have its edges whipstitched with cording and yarn as a finishing touch to add durability.

Despite the simplicity of the basic method, highly intricate designs can be created with it. Using a multitude of dyeing techniques to produce unusual effects, or various hooking methods to create realistic shading, or different widths of wool to achieve a primitive or formal style, today's rug hookers have gone beyond making strictly utilitarian floor coverings to also make wallhangings, vests, lampshades, purses, pictorials, portraits, and more. Some have incorporated other kinds of needlework into their hooked rugs to fashion unique and fascinating fiber art that's been shown in museums, exhibits, and galleries throughout the world.

For a good look at what contemporary rug hookers are doing with yesteryear's craft—or to learn how to hook your own rug—pick up a copy of *Rug Hooking* magazine, or visit our web site at *www.rughookingonline.com*. Within the world of rug hooking—and *Rug Hooking* magazine—you'll find there's a style to suit every taste and a growing community of giving, gracious fiber artists who will welcome you to their gatherings.

—Ginny Stimmel

ABOUT THE *Publisher*

Rug Hooking magazine welcomes you to the rug hooking community. Since 1989 *Rug Hooking* has served thousands of rug hookers around the world with its instructional, illustrated articles on dyeing, designing, color planning, hooking techniques, and more. Each issue of the magazine contains color photographs of beautiful rugs old and new, profiles of teachers, designers, and fellow rug hookers, and announcements of workshops, exhibits, and gatherings.

Rug Hooking has responded to its readers' demands for more inspiration and information by establishing an inviting, informative website at *www.rughooking online.com* and by publishing a number of books on this fiber art. Along with how-to pattern books, *Rug Hooking* has produced the competition-based book series *A Celebration of Hand-Hooked Rugs*, now in its 17th year.

The hand-hooked rugs you'll see in *A Celebration of Hand-Hooked Rugs XVI* represent just a fragment of the incredible art that is being produced today by women and men of all ages. For more information on rug hooking and *Rug Hooking* magazine, call or write to us at the address on page 4.

ᴬᴺ *Introduction*

Rug hooking is seeing an incredible surge in popularity. Many new people are joining guilds and groups across the United States and Canada. This interest has spurred rug hooking designers to create new patterns, write books and articles, and develop classes that inspire another generation of excited rug hookers. The Internet has opened up a whole new world of inquiring minds looking for ideas and information on making rug hooking a vital part of their world.

We want to be part of that exciting new growth. This book is a tangible extension of our love and respect for this great craft and those who practice it. We have been hooking rugs for many years and are always looking for ways to incorporate rug hooking with other handicrafts for uses in our homes and as a way of self expression. Let it be known, however, our first love is a hooked RUG. To us, a rug is the purest expression of this craft, practiced by our ancestors with love to make their homes a better place.

That being said, we enjoy applying the techniques of rug hooking to all kinds of dimensional forms. After reading and collecting most of the books available on the subject of rug hooking, we found a peculiar lack of information on project-based rug hooking. Many of us are out there doing small projects or applying rug hooking to pillows, dolls, purses, and table runners. We contacted some of the best designers and teachers and challenged them to create projects that experienced and beginning rug hookers would enjoy making. This collection of hooked projects is a tribute to their creativity.

There are some assumptions we are going to make about our readers. We assume you already know the basics of rug hooking and sewing. If not, there are a variety of great books on the market that can help you with the fundamentals. We are also going to assume you have done some crafting and can wield a glue gun, scissors, and paintbrush without fear. Hopefully, the patterns and instructions in this book are easy to read and follow and will make sense to you.

We hope these projects are a springboard for your imagination. Once you have made a purse, design your own! Change the colors and feel free to adapt the ideas to your specific needs and desires. The information and techniques presented in this book are guidelines for your rug hooking adventures. The possibilities are endless as this book so readily demonstrates. Pick out a project and get hooking! Enjoy.

—*Jenny and Lisa*

ABOUT THE *Authors*

The Potted Pear

We started our rug hooking business in 2001. It seemed like a natural progression to extend our love of rug hooking into a business partnership. We design patterns; write books, catalogs and articles; dye wool and yarn; develop dye formulas; and teach classes.

Handwork is part of our shared history. As little girls, we both grew up in homes where sewing and crafting were important activities. As we grew older, we tried all the arts and crafts in school and at home with our mothers and grandmothers. It is no wonder we share a strong love for fiber arts. It is in our blood.

We want to thank our families for putting up with all those wool fuzzies around the house and for not being disappointed when wool is cooking in the kitchen and not supper. A special thanks goes to Sally Korte and Alice Strebel of Kindred Spirits. Your friendship, inspiration, and encouragement mean the world to us.

Jenny Rupp

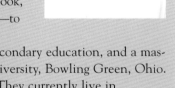

Jenny's rug hooking obsession started in 1992 in Atlanta, Georgia, where she learned how to hook at a folk art shop and moved on to weekly classes with a teacher. In 1996 she helped to establish the Sauder Village rug event in Archbold, Ohio. This rug event brings together teachers, vendors, and special exhibits to the Midwest.

Jenny has hooked every kind of rug item you can imagine: purses, pillows, runners, rugs, footstool covers, chair pads, chair backs, ornaments, and dolls. "It is in my dolls that I can best express my sense of humor and view of the world. I strongly encourage you to use this book, not simply as a pattern book, but as a springboard for diving into your own ideas. Don't be afraid to try—to incorporate your experience into your projects," she adds.

Jenny has a bachelor's degree in education, a master's degree in secondary education, and a master's degree in guidance and counseling from Bowling Green State University, Bowling Green, Ohio. She married the boy next door in 1981, and they have one daughter. They currently live in Cincinnati, Ohio.

Lisa Yeago

Lisa Yeago began her love of needlework as a child. After trying everything from crocheting and knitting to cross-stitch she began to teach quilting in 1990 at a small quilt shop in Cincinnati, Ohio. One of her quilting students suggested that she attend a rug hooking meeting. She attended this first meeting in 1995 and has been hooking ever since. Lisa has attended many rug workshops and camps and has studied with a variety of teachers. In 2001 she, along with partner Jenny Rupp, formed The Potted Pear.

Lisa currently resides in Cincinnati, Ohio, with her husband Tim, daughter Sarah, and son Nathan. She has a bachelor's degree in music, a master's degree in music, and an MBA. She works part-time as a commercial real estate consultant but still finds time for her love—rug hooking.

Polka Dot Pillow

LOOPDEELOO RUG DESIGNS BY KATHERINE PORTER

For this pillow I used my grandmother's old wool blanket as the backing. The blanket had a large monogram of her initials which was slightly worn and threadbare but still maintained a certain charm and elegance. I used the monogram section of the blanket as the back of the pillow. The corded edge is made with hand-dyed, variegated 3-ply yarn.

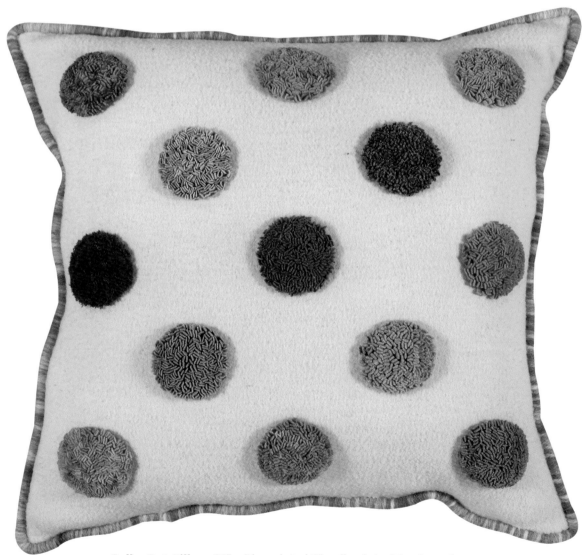

Polka Dot Pillow, 20" with sculpted 2" polka dots, #6-cut wool on wool blanket backing. Designed and hooked by Katherine Porter, Chardon, Ohio, 2005.

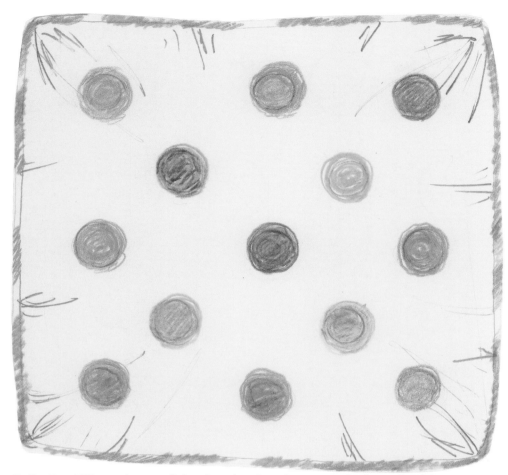

Polka Dot Pillow color pencil drawing showing placement of color polka dots.

Plan Your Color

Make a few copies of the pattern to sketch your color plan. Try a few different ideas. In my pillow each dot is a different color although some are close in hue. Orange, warm red, and mauve predominate, while olive greens and gold are secondary.

Transfer the Pattern

Enlarge this pattern to 20" x 20". Mark a 20" x 20" outline on the wool with a pencil, being careful to stay on the grain line. Pin the pattern in place and transfer the design. Choose a transfer method which will not leave a permanent mark on the wool. I used a dressmaker's tracing paper and wheel.

Hooking the Dots

Cut each strip of wool with a #6 cutter. Use a finer hook (#2 or #3) as this will break through the backing more easily. Start in the middle of each dot and pull loops up high, at least 1". Work in a random manner around the circle, tapering your loops to about $1/2$" at the outside edge. Random hooking (as opposed to even circles) will give better coverage in the end. Be sure to cover the whole area right up to the line.

Sculpting the Dots

With small, sharp, pointed scissors clip all the loops open. Trim carefully and gradually until you have a domed shape. Be careful not to cut away too much too quickly. When finished, lightly vacuum with a brush attachment to remove wool clippings.

Making Corded Edge

Place cord on the wrong side of pillow face just outside the edge line. Wrap edge of pil-

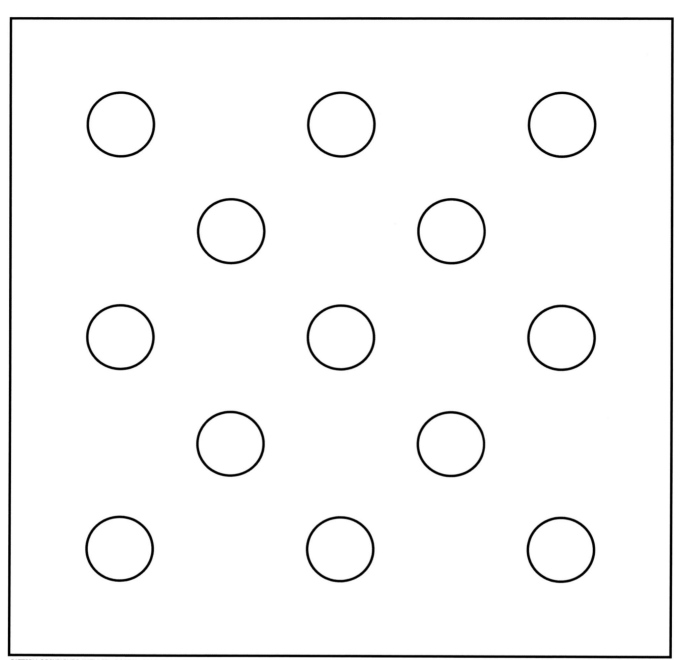

Make a few copies of the pattern to sketch your color plan. Try a few different ideas.

low face tightly around cording towards the wrong side. Pin along the edge line of the pattern making sure the cording is to the outside of this line. Whipstitch along a straight edge (not a corner) about 1" from the cut end of cording. Whipstitch around the cord using a bent tapestry needle and 3-ply yarn. This is similar to the method of finishing a rug with yarn. Work the corners carefully. Keep your whipstitches close together to cover the backing. Remember this trim will be seen from the back also. When it is stitched all the way around, cut the cording so it will overlap by 1". Whipstitch this overlapping section to complete the trim. If the corded edge is wavy and twisted at this point, press it with a steam iron and damp cloth being careful not to press the polka dots.

Attaching Front and Back

Place right sides together. Open the seam allowance on the pillow face so the cording is to the inside. Carefully pin pattern lines of front and back together. This may be a little difficult because of the cording. Stretch your wool a bit to make the corners match. Leave a 12" opening centered on one side for stuffing the pillow. Begin at one side of this opening and stitch around the pillow by hand using a backstitch. Make sure to stitch very close to the corded trim so you will not see a gap on the right side.

Finishing

Trim edges to $^1/_2$" of seam line. Do not clip corners. Turn right side out. Steam around edges with a damp cloth again, if needed. Insert pillow form. You may want to stuff a little fiberfill into each corner. Blind stitch across opening to complete the pillow.

Designer's Tip—Color Planning Your Project

No matter how simple the color scheme may be, it's always a good idea to make a color sketch of the pattern. I like using color pencils because you can sketch lightly at first then build up the color using different shades to approximate the richness of wool. If the first idea doesn't work out try something else.

Other Creative Options

- Instead of sculpting, hook the dots in your preferred cut of wool.

- Make all dots the same color on a multi-colored wool background.

- Choose five different colors for the dots and line them up.

- On the back, use a beautiful coordinating print or woven fabric, a piece of "painted" wool, a section of a worn paisley shawl, or some other antique fabric.

- For trim, make cording out of bias cut strips of wool wrapped around the cotton cord or simply use a ready made trim.

- Have fun and be creative!

No matter how simple the color scheme may be, it's always a good idea to make a color sketch of the pattern.

Remember: As with mixing paint, use the complementary color to dull or dirty a hue. ●

ARTIST: KATHERINE PORTER

As a fabric designer for over 20 years, needle arts enthusiast Katherine Porter was thrilled to discover rug hooking about eight years ago at a local fair. In 2002 Katherine began selling her patterns and the following year produced a catalog called "Loopdeeloo." Her designs spring from a lifelong love of antique textiles and are inspired by a variety of historic styles. Wide-cut rug hooking can give "traditional" a fresh, modern look—a clean contemporary feel is her goal. For further information contact: Katherine Porter, 9985 Auburn Road, Chardon, Ohio 44024; telephone (440) 286-4356; fax (440) 286-1759; email: loopdeeloorugs@yahoo.com.

Table Scraps

BY SALLY KALLIN OF PINE ISLAND PRIMITIVES, PINE ISLAND, MINNESOTA

As children we were all told to "clean our plates," but sometimes there were still leftovers. In rug hooking we also end up with leftovers. This table runner project is a fun way to use up those scraps of wool to create something beautiful. Hooking with my old cut strips was like seeing old friends again, as I was reminded of other projects from the past. If you are new to hooking and don't have a basket of cut strips, you can collect strips from other rug hookers and the rug will be a reminder of your friends.

This pattern is meant to be unpretentious. The stars are crooked and the diamond shapes are not perfect. This all adds to the charm of the piece. So leave perfectionism behind, throw caution to the wind, and have fun hooking this primitive table runner.

Table Scraps is a great pattern to customize to any size or shape you need.

This one is 13" x 46¹/₂" and each square is 4" x 4". I chose to use this as a table runner, but it would make a great piano bench cover or any other piece that requires a custom size. You can add or subtract squares or change the size of the squares altogether. Just remember that a piece changes size as it is hooked. In the hooking process this piece shrunk 1" in

Table Scraps, 46¹/₂" x 13", #8-cut wool on linen. Designed and hooked by Sally Kallin, Pine Island, Minnesota, 2005.

WHAT YOU NEED:

Below is a list of the wool I used to hook *Table Scraps*, mostly with #8 ($^1/_4$")
cut strips, although some of my scraps were already cut in different widths.
The colors I have chosen for *Table Scraps* are just a suggestion. Please feel
free to make it your own by choosing the colors that you love.

Item	Color	Amount
Background	Several shades of dark colors (black, blue, brown etc...)	1$^1/_4$ yard total
Stars	Various Gold Textures	$^3/_4$ yard total
Outline	Red	$^1/_4$ yard
Antique Paisley		8" x 12" piece
Diamonds & Stripes	Variety of colors	lots of leftover cut strips

Note: If you can't find paisley or are skeptical about using it, substitute a
high-contrast, small-scale textured fabric.

length and the width remained the
same. If you are looking for a particular finished size, keep checking
the measurements as you go. If the
piece changes size as you hook it,
adjust the length of the stripes on
the ends of the runner to meet your
needs.

Drawing Table Scraps

Start with the backing of your choice
23" x 57" or larger. Measure to find the
center in both directions. Then measure five 4" sections out from the vertical
centerline (see diagram) in both directions. Measure 2" on either side of the
horizontal centerline to get the center

PHOTOGRAPH BY BILL BISHOP/IMPACT XPOZURES

horizontal center line

VERTICAL CENTER LINE

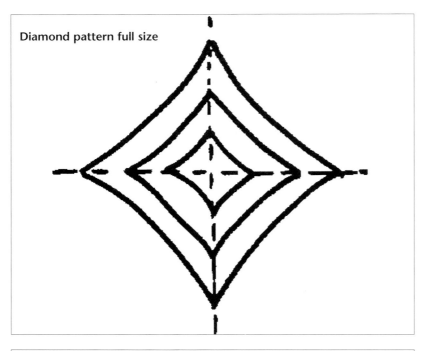

Diamond pattern full size

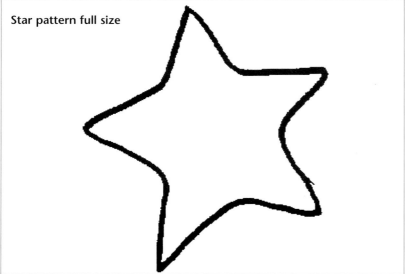

Star pattern full size

row of 4"squares. Add another 4" section above and below that. With a sharp pencil complete the squares by drawing lines between the same threads of the backing the whole length of each line. (This is drawing on the "straight of the grain.") A straight pattern is necessary to produce a straight and square finished rug. You should end up with a total of 30 squares. At each short end add 2³/₄" for the stripes. The piece should now measure 12" x 45¹/₂". To get the extra ¹/₂" all around, just hook two rows of a #8-cut strip for the border.

Trace the diamond and star shapes to make templates. Using a permanent marker, trace the curved diamond shapes at each intersection of your squares. Line up the

dashed line on the pattern with the pencil lines on your backing. Make partial diamonds at the edges and corners. The curved diamond shapes create a circle in the center of each 4" square. Trace a star in the center of each circle, turning the star in different directions to get a playful pattern. Draw over the pencil lines with a Sharpie marker to connect the lines between the diamonds. To keep the edges of the backing from raveling, it is necessary to serge, zigzag, or simply tape them. If this all sounds too complicated, the pattern can be ordered from Pine Island Primitives. It is available on either monk's cloth or linen and includes a color photograph.

The Color Plan

This table runner is going on a harvest table in my dining room. I love antique rugs and the look that is achieved by using what you have. I seldom hook with specific colors that match my décor. I believe that if you hook what you like, it will work in your house. The beauty of using leftover strips for this project is that the same wools may have been used in other hooked pieces in the house so this project will fit in comfortably.

This color plan started with the dark backgrounds. I wanted it to have some black in it as well as lots of small bits of other colors. I knew that I wanted something dark and neutral so all of the wonderful colors of the scraps would show up. The gold stars were chosen to contrast with the dark backgrounds and to keep the piece warm. For the outline, a medium value red was chosen to complement the dark backgrounds and the various colors in the diamonds. It also picks up the red in the antique paisley used in the centers of the diamonds. I have to admit, this rug was pretty drab before I hooked the diamonds and the stripes. The hit-or-miss style and mix of colors and textures is what makes this rug come alive. It was fun to get out the scrap basket and play with the various colored strips.

Attention was paid to the placement of the different backgrounds to balance throughout the piece. I avoided using my lightest star color against my darkest background color to prevent that area from having too much contrast and becoming too important.

The striped border was added at the end because I felt the piece needed more color. It is advantageous to have extra backing around the rug so you have the opportunity to make changes to the design without running out of space.

Hooking Table Scraps

When working on a rug, I like to hook a small area to test out all of the colors; this helps prevent ripping out later. In this rug, I hooked a small section of outline, four stars and backgrounds, part of the border, and a few diamonds. When I was happy with the combination I went on to hook the rest of the rug.

I started by hooking the red outline first. Next, the stars were hooked using six different gold's. Remember to hook inside the lines to keep a good shape on your stars. The backgrounds were hooked with eight different dark colors. In each star or background I used all the same wool. This helps create a nice variety of lights and darks. If the stars or backgrounds were hooked with mixing the wools in each group, it would have caused them to all look the same.

The outside border was hooked next with a dark plaid. When I have a design element that runs into the border, I like to get the border hooked to keep the edges of the rug straight. The diamond shapes were hooked next from the outside in, filling in the centers with antique paisley. The size of these diamonds is set up to hook two rows of a #8 cut and then fill in the center. If you use a narrower cut, there would be more rows. I

Designer's Tip: How to Hook with Antique Paisley

Antique paisley is to a hooked rug as jewelry is to a great outfit. The busy texture and rich colors add a sparkle to your hooked pieces. It takes a rug from great to spectacular.

There is some controversy about cutting up valuable antique paisleys. I recommend only using the pieces that already have some damage to them, but still have structural integrity. Most of the paisleys are over 100 years old, so they can be fragile or shred when you hook with them. Once you use them, I think you will see that they are worth the extra effort.

A few hints in using paisleys:
1. Cut by hand or with a cutter in a #8 or wider.
2. Cut in the direction of the "strings" on the back.
3. Only cut the strips that are going to be used immediately.
4. Carefully hook with a large shanked hook to open up the backing, and so you can grab the whole strip and avoid stressing the paisley.
5. Hook with front side up (the side without the strings).
6. Hook other wool around paisley ASAP.

chose strips of wool that would create contrast next to the paisley. The stripes on the short ends of the rug were hooked last.

Finishing

The edge of this rug was finished by whipping with wool yarn, catching a small amount of the binding tape with each stitch. This way the binding is securely attached and you get to skip a step in finishing. A narrow whipped edge is created that does not detract from the design of the rug. After the whipping was finished, the other edge of the binding tape was tacked down using button and craft thread.

I hope *Table Scraps* inspires you to use up some of your leftovers to create a beautiful rug. ●

ARTIST: SALLY KALLIN

Sally Kallin is the owner of Pine Island Primitives. She lives on a hobby farm in Pine Island, Minnesota with her husband Keith, her daughter Hannah, several cats, three horses, and her dog—Jack "the German Wool Hound." She teaches at her farm and at workshops and camps across the country. Her rug hooking patterns can be ordered through her catalog or purchased in her wool-filled shop. You can reach her at (507) 356-2908, e-mail at rugs@pitel.net, or visit her website www.pineislandprimitives.com. Pine Island Primitives, 16369 County 11 Blvd., Pine Island, MN 55963. See more of Sally's rugs in A Celebration of Hand-Hooked Rugs XII *and the January/February 2003 and November/December 2006 issues of* Rug Hooking.

Vanity Stool

BY KIM NIXON

Making hooked rug pieces into three dimensional stool coverings has been a focus of my work and teaching for the last five years. For some time I had been comtemplating sewing the backing pieces together to create the rounded stool shape before hooking begins. This way the hooking can be laid in neat rows along the seam with no gap in the backing. The best thing about this process is that when the hooking is completed, the piece is ready to put on the stool, making the project almost complete. The downside of this project is that it involved mathematical terms that I had to look up. Also, when the sides were hooked, the piece wasn't going to lay flat on the frame. If you hate not hooking flat, substitute purchased fabric for the sides—that way the project will be done faster.

This pattern has very simple shapes, so it is how we color and define these shapes that make it a piece of art. Integrating the background with the motif of the fleur de lis was intentional and accomplished by breaking down the edges of the motif with tonal values that blend into the background color. Adding dark highlights as subtle patterning also relates the background to the darker fleur de lis. The softness of the coloring and using some as-is textured wools sets a contemplative tone that relates also to a softening of focus for its use as a vanity stool.

Initially this stool pattern was intended to have a star on top. At the last minute I changed the design to the fleur de lis since it is a motif that has been a part of my life, and it lends a more elegant feel to the stool. Interestingly, Hurricane Katrina hit the Gulf Coast and caused damage in New Orleans as I was working on it. I grew up in New Orleans and spent summers on the Gulf. This area of the world is founded on a genteel idea that one moves slowly, because it is so incredibly hot, and enjoying worldly pleasures is a wonderful means for survival in such a tropical place. The fleur de lis is a French symbol that is a sign of sophistication or pretentiousness. But, by using it on everyday embellishment, it becomes a bohemian idea of culture for the masses. It's meaning is "flower of lily." While the flower reminds us of something gone forever, it also calls attention to all the displaced people who will carry New Orleans' future in their hearts.

Getting Started:

Trace the patterns on the appropriate sized pieces of backing making sure that the side piece is lined up on the grain of the backing fabric and that all the darts are marked. (**Figure 1**) The top piece of backing needs to have the circle pattern centered so there is enough room on all sides to stretch it on your frame. (**Figure 2**) Once the two pieces

Fleur de lis Vanity Stool, $17^1/_2$"
circumference, #9-cut wool on linen.
Designed and hooked by Kim Nixon,
Maryville, Tennesseee, 2005

WHAT YOU NEED:

- Two pieces of quality backing fabric which will not stretch such as Cushing linen, rug warp, or Scottish burlap

- Top piece—21" x 24" (enlarge pattern 200%)

- Sidepiece—13" x 60" (enlarge pattern 200%)

- Wool for hooking

- Tacky glue

- Spray adhesive

- Fray Check©

- Upholstery braid (gimp), $1^3/_4$ yard length

- 4" thick high–density foam, cut in a circle measuring $17^1/_2$" (or a piece large enough to cut your own)

- $17^1/_2$" round circle cut in $^3/_4$" plywood (painted black on one side)

- $15^1/_2$" wrought iron legs (available through Kim's studio, Under the Rug)

EQUIPMENT:

- Sewing machine to sew backing pieces together

- Electric kitchen knife for cutting foam (if you don't have one, have it cut by a foam dealer)

- Staple gun

- Small hooking frame with gripper strips

are sewn together the excess on that top piece of backing needs to be stretched on the frame. The side piece of backing needs to have only a $1^1/_2$" seam allowance on the top (the side with the darts) so trace it $1^1/_2$" from one long edge of the side piece of backing. The lines that divide the side sections into quarters are important to mark. They are the lines that will match up with the quarter lines in the top circle when sewn together.

Next, sew all the darts (**Figure 3**) taking time to make sure that they are

stitched uniformly and pressed flat to equally divide them on each side of the dart. In this way, the dart seam won't be too much to one side making it hard to hook on that side. (**Figure 4**)

On the sidepiece, sew the end seam together to form a large ring. Sew a zigzag strip $^1/_4$" from the bottom edge of the side-piece. This will help with unraveling once the top is stapled on the stool.

Now you are ready to sew the two pieces together. Putting right sides together and matching up the quarter marks of the

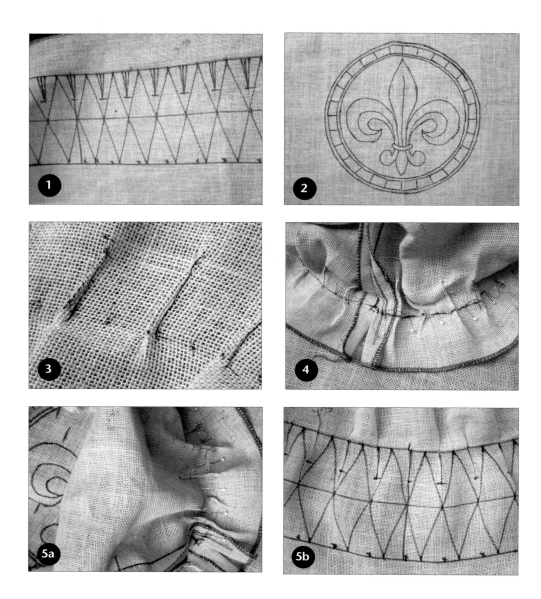

pattern, pin them together. Then pin within each quarter section lining up the seam lines around the circle. Sew this seam and check to see that it lines up correctly (**Figure 5**). I used a good sewing thread on my machine with a basic stitch length setting making sure it was knotted well at the beginning and end of the seam. Do not trim off the excess top circle backing fabric. It will help you in hooking the top.

Note: Because backing fabric unravels so quickly with handling, I usually serge or zigzag all seam allowances and all edges. It is always better to avoid this problem if you can.

When making a stool top, it is something that needs to fit an exact shape and size. To that end, I recommend that you

start to size from the beginning. The pattern pieces have been sized to fit the $17^1/2$" circular piece of plywood. It is never too early to have the plywood and foam ready to fit the pattern. First, take the foam rubber and trace the wooden circle on it (**Figure 6**). Then using an electric kitchen knife, cut around the drawn circle making sure to hold the knife at a 90-degree angle so the sides of the foam are perpendicular to the plywood base. (**Figure 7**) When the circle is the way you want it, take the knife and trim around the top edge for a more rounded look to the stool. (**Figure 8**) Now is the time to take your pattern and fit around the circular foam and pull it down. It will have all the excess backing pieces, but you can get a feel for the circumference. The pattern should

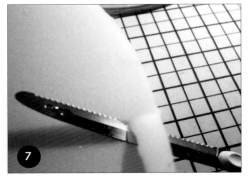

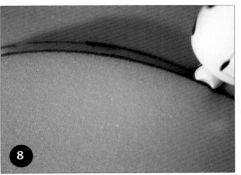

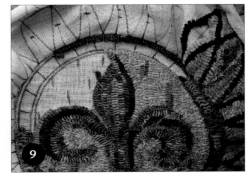

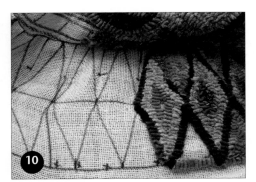

1. Fleur de lis side pattern on linen backing

2. Fleur de lis pattern top on linen backing

3. Side darts detail shot

4. Pinning top to side, evenly spacing between darts

5a & 5b. Sewing the top to the side panel

6. Marking the foam for stool top

7. Cutting the foam with electric knife

8. Shaping the foam pad

9. Hooking the top

10. Hooking the side

11. Hooking next to the seam

be a little big because it is sized to be taken up by the hooking.

Begin hooking the piece, as you would normally work. Hooking the top circle is fairly easy because the untrimmed piece of top will stretch over most common sized frames. (**Figure 9**) A small hooking frame is listed in the equipment list, since when hooking the side piece it is not something that lays flat anymore. I used an Appleton frame, pulling the backing tight up and down, and then pulling as best as I could on the sides to get a fairly flat work surface for hooking each diamond. (**Figure 10**) If you move it for each diamond, it isn't that hard. Hook going up and down around each of the darts on the sidepiece. Using a hoop to hook this pattern might be more difficult.

The beauty of going to the trouble of sewing two pieces of backing together before hooking is that you can hook right up on the seam around the rounded top, (**Figure 11**) shifting the seam allowances out of the way so they aren't caught in your loops. In fact, put a row of hooking around the seam, and build the border on the top piece inward with the rows of hooking, so it works out to the size strips you are using.

Size the pattern to the foam and board top as you hook. Rug hooking is very forgiving; if the backing is too big, any extra can easily be eased in. The pattern is sized to have the pattern fit snugly over the foam once it is hooked. It should start out a little big but be absorbed by the hooking into being slightly snug. The top should also just

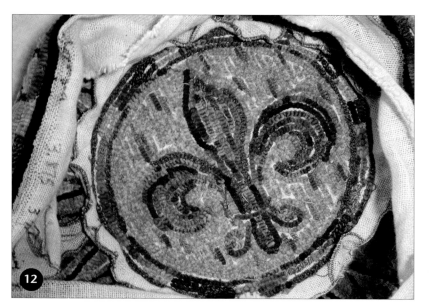

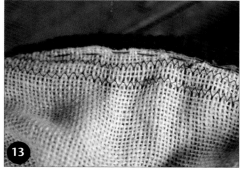

12. Trimming the back side of the pattern

13. Stapling the rug top to the board

14. Running a bead of glue to attach a decorative braid

sit down over the foam rubber. It will be pulled down to cover the side edge of the bottom board. If the piece is hooking up too big, then work your way back and take in some darts along the bottom edge starting at each quadrant. If the piece is too small then consider cutting the board and foam circle down to 17" in diameter. Be aware that the

legs for this stool need a minimum of a 17" to attach.

Complete all the hooking on the piece and press the top and sides. Be patient when pressing the sides, keeping that rounded shape. Notice any holidays that need more wool because once the top is upholstered, you won't have access to the back to fill them in. When you feel that the top is a good fit, then trim out all the excess backing pieces inside the top, not along the bottom edge. (**Figure 12**) Again use a serger or zigzag to edge them so they don't unravel.

Upholstering the hooked top of the stool is very easy. Line up the quarter marks on the sidepiece to general quarter marks on the bottom board. I use a spray fabric adhesive to anchor the foam on the unpainted side of the board to keep it in place, but the foam is heavy and dense enough to not really shift on its own. Using a staple gun, start out by anchoring the four-quarter marks of the circle, stapling one and then stapling its opposite diameter point. Pull the hooked edge of the sidepiece to where the last row of hooking rolls to the bottom side of the board, making sure to cover the board well. The staples need to be within $1/4$" of the hooked edge, because the backing is going to be trimmed to $3/8$" in order to attach a

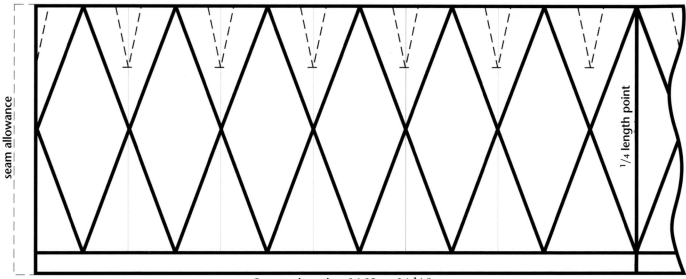

¹/₄ total length

seam allowance

¹/₄ length point

Quarter length = 14.13 or 14 ¹/₈"
Total Length of side strip = 56.52" or 56 ³⁴/₆₄". Enlarge pattern to 13" x 60" for use.

decorative braid finish to hide it. (**Figure 13**) Proceed around the circle by finding the center of each of the quarter sections and stapling there, being mindful of easing the backing between the staples. The easiest way to do this is to staple the center point between the last two staples already placed, so you are always easing between two points. In this way the circle won't be pulled off center. The backing should be nice and smooth on the top, since the foam is compressed a little bit by pulling against it to anchor the backing.

Trim the backing to the zigzagged line of stitches to equal about ³/₈" or as close to the staples as possible. Use a good fabric glue to squirt out a bead to cover the edge of

the backing all the way around the circle. Be careful not to get glue on the loops. (**Figure 14**) Place the upholstery braid over the glue neatly covering the backing and the staples. Here the bottom board is painted black and the braid is black for a uniform finish that matches the legs. The hooked edge of the stool is also hooked with a black row for a simple elegant finish.

Let all the glue dry and attach the legs for a complete stool. The wrought iron legs are a triangle cut from a 6" piece of metal. Center a 6" square on the bottom of the bottom board then you will have the placement for your legs. To attach, use wood screws that are about an inch long. ●

Designer Tip:

Always think about the whole piece when making a dimensional piece of art. The legs and the finishing need to relate to the design or at least not compete with it. Everything added is another element in the whole piece down to the way you sign your name.

ARTIST: KIM NIXON

For the last 12 years traditional rug hooking has offered Kim Nixon the opportunity to combine an old love of fiber with a painter's experience of design and color. She has a MFA in fine art and 25 years experience as a painter that she brings to making rugs. Designing for footstools requires three-dimensional thinking and problem solving ability to upholster it to the stool. Since 2000, Kim has run her own business called Under the Rug to market her designs, rugs, and stools. To view a portfolio of her work and Under the Rug designs, please visit her website, www.undertherug.com. Stool kits available upon request. Kim Nixon, 2117 Ludwick Drive, Maryville, TN 37803; (865) 681-8733 or email at k_nixon@bellsouth.net

Miss Liberty Hooked Rug

BY BEVERLY GOODRICH

As a folk artist with an interest in Americana, I carved Miss Liberty several years ago as a change from my specialty, which was folky Santas. I now express myself in wool with rug hooking and penny rugs since carpal tunnel halted my wood carving. I felt Miss Liberty was a subject that could be created with texture in this form of fiber arts since she really seemed to have something else to say.

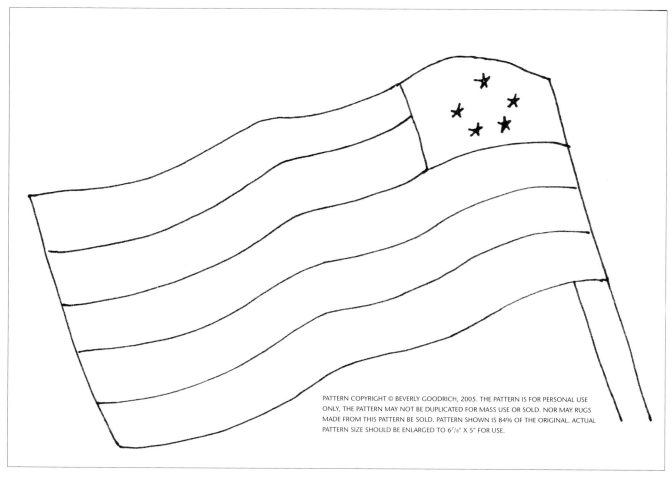

WHAT YOU NEED:

WOOL:

- Red—$1/8$ yard for flag and dress

- Blue—$1/16$ yard for flag and dress

- Cream or off-white—$1/8$ yard for flag, cuffs, neckline, and dress

- Skin color—$1/16$ yard for arms and face

- Dark brown—3"x 15" piece for hair and eyes

- Rose—1 strip for cheeks

- Darker rose—1 strip for lips

- Black, 3 or 4 various—$3/8$ yard for eyebrows, nose, and background

- Gold tweed—2" x 15" piece for flagpole

- Backing—15" x 23" on linen

- Basic hooking supplies

Miss Liberty, 11" x 19" with various sizes of wool strips on linen. Adapted from an antique piece of folk art. Hooked by Beverly Goodrich, Gainesville, Georgia, 2005.

PATTERN COPYRIGHT © BEVERLY GOODRICH, 2005. THE PATTERN IS FOR PERSONAL USE ONLY, THE PATTERN MAY NOT BE DUPLICATED FOR MASS USE OR SOLD. NOR MAY RUGS MADE FROM THIS PATTERN BE SOLD. PATTERN SHOWN IS 65% OF THE ORIGINAL. ACTUAL PATTERN SIZE SHOULD BE ENLARGED TO 7¹/₈" X 10¹/₂" FOR USE.

Hooking Instructions

1. Trace pattern onto linen by laying the backing over the pattern. Trace onto backing with a black permanent marker. *Miss Liberty* should be placed in the center of the 11" x 19" edge lines.

2. To hook *Miss Liberty*, start with the face. Cut the strips for the facial features a little narrower. To do this, use scissors to cut the strip right down the middle. For the features I used brown for the eyes,

black for the eyebrows and nose line, rose for the cheeks, and a darker rose for the lips. Hook the skin-colored wool around the features. Tip: After hooking in the skin color, use your hook to arrange the loops around the features. Don't be afraid to use your scissors to snip at the loops a bit so the features can be seen. Use the photo as a guide for hooking the rest of *Miss Liberty*.

After hooking in the skin color, use your hook to arrange the loops around the features. Don't be afraid to use your scissors to snip at the loops a bit so the features can be seen.

3. To hook the background take your various black wool strips and cut them. Hook one or two lines around the edge of the design. Then hook around *Miss Liberty* and her flag. Continue hooking around her and fill in. If you mix the black strips up in a bag, you can pull them out at random and hook them in for a mottled black background.

4. For detail you may want to highlight around *Miss Liberty's* dark brown hair so it stands out against the background. Take a piece of cream wool and hand cut it thin, and then hook in around the hair and background. It may be a tight fit, but it makes a nice little line. You can do the same thing on her sleeve by cutting a black strip thin and hooking it between the white cuff and her arm.

5. Steam the mat and allow it to completely dry before finishing. See the final chapter on finishing for instructions. *Miss Liberty* was finished with a whipped yarn edge and then twill tape. ●

Pictured above is Beverly Goodrich's *Lady Liberty* both as a wood carving and a penny rug. For more information about the penny rug, contact Beverly at (770) 287–8617.

ARTIST: BEVERLY GOODRICH

Beverly is a folk art painter and was a wood carver until she developed carpal tunnel syndrome. (She carved the wooden Miss Liberty in 1993.) She started hooking rugs in 1992 and has found a real passion for the fiber art. She also incorporates needle felting and penny rugs into table runners, purses, eyeglass and needle cases, etc. She lives with her husband, Garth, in Gainesville, Georgia, and has three daughters and five grandchildren.

Handbag Slip Cover

BY CINDI GAY

Do you look longingly at beautifully finished hooked handbags but cringe at the idea of all that finishing work? Does the dream of doing it yourself end with the contents of your handbag strewn across the sidewalk? To display your hooking as mobile art is a great way to explain to others how you spend every free moment. But who is going to explain to you the advanced finishing techniques needed? If the idea of making a handbag is too much for you, keep it simple and hook a handbag slip cover for an existing item instead. As with a slipcover for your sofa, the original item will remain intact. Your hooking covers the highly visible areas only and provides a fresh, colorful, and custom new look. Read the instructions here for two simple handbags I completed and apply the methods to your favorite style of handbag.

What to Look For

Cover almost anything that tickles your imagination. For this project I used an existing small purse and an expandable pencil pouch. Apply a slipcover to the flat area on your telephone or camera case, add color to your PDA cover, and style to your eyeglass case. Apply these ideas to any item that you wish to embellish.

Look for items with a flat open area and avoid closure mechanisms that pierce the flap. A smooth flap is the easiest style

HARD EYEGLASS CASE

A hard eyeglass case is impossible to stitch into. Hook a slightly smaller area and attach the finished piece to the top with glue or Velcro. Use the sew-on style for the hooked piece and the stick-on style for your item. Be sure to attach the hooks to one side and the loops to the other.

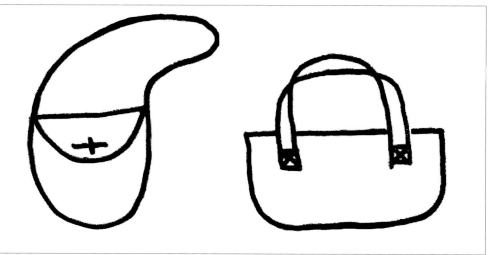

Avoid styles where the closure pierces the flap and the handles attach to the side of the bag.

Back view of flower design purse.

to cover. Stay away from the areas with buttonholes or where the straps attach. When the hooking is bent, you can often see the backing through the loops. Avoid this problem by covering the curved area with a flat piece of wool instead of hooking. But if you have your heart set on hooking that area, be sure to pack the loops in the section that will be curved to keep the backing covered even when it is bent over the area.

Drawing the Pattern

A paper pattern that is the same size as the area intended for covering will need to be created. If you have trouble with the paper ripping, try a piece of inexpensive fabric,

Circle design handbag slipcover. Designed and hooked by Cindi Gay, Pemberville, Ohio, 2005.

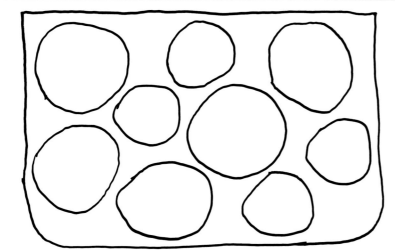

PATTERN COPYRIGHT © CINDI GAY, 2005. THE PATTERN IS FOR PERSONAL USE ONLY, THE PATTERN MAY NOT BE DUPLICATED FOR MASS USE OR SOLD. NOR MAY RUGS MADE FROM THIS PATTERN BE SOLD. PATTERN SHOWN IS 39% OF THE ORIGINAL. ACTUAL PATTERN SIZE SHOULD BE ENLARGED TO 9^1/2" X 6^1/2" FOR USE.

Circle design

such as muslin instead. Trace the outline of the area to be covered. Lay the item with the side to be covered up, if possible. If not, flip the paper over after tracing it. For instance, it is easier to trace the pencil pouch with the zippers up, but the correct shape and the side we want to cover is found by tracing with the smooth side up. Trace it with the zippers up and then flip the pattern over. To verify that it is right, cut along the pattern line. Place the cut out pattern on your item in the proper position. Flip it over if it does not fit correctly. Put an "X" on the exposed side of the pattern.

Many mass produced items vary slightly in size and shape from one side to the other even though they appear symmetrical.

If you are able to trace the flap while it is flat, be sure to check the pattern on the purse with the flap in the closed position. Extend the length of the pattern if needed in order to cover everything. Slightly bigger is better than slightly smaller. As you hook, test fit the hooked piece to the item often. Your style of hooking and the backing used may distort the shape.

Now think ahead to the type of finishing you will use. If you whip or crochet the edge, reduce the area to be hooked by the approximate size of your finish. Everyone will have a different measurement depending on the method or the backing. If unsure, measure the edge of a rug finished with your chosen method on the same kind of backing. If your edge takes up ^{1}/4" then reduce the size of your pattern by ^{1}/4" wherever you will have a finished edge. Cut your pattern on this new line. If you intend to simply turn back the edge, skip this step.

Choose Your Design

I chose simple designs that used up the scraps from my prior hooking. Adapt any design that suits so keep it simple or prepare

Star design handbag slipcover. Designed and hooked by Cindi Gay, Pemberville, Ohio, 2005.

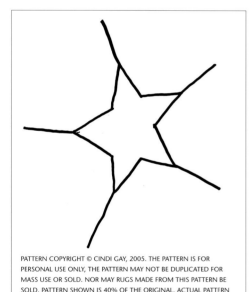

Star design

to use smaller cuts. Size the design to fit into the tracing made in the prior step. To use the star design, enlarge the star pattern to the desired size and extend the lines to the outer edge. The simple circle design is fun because the shapes only need to suggest circles. They do not have to be drawn with a compass or hooked perfectly. Using colored paper cut irregular circles of several sizes and move them around the tracing created in the prior step until you like the layout. Add or subtract circles as needed to fill the pat-

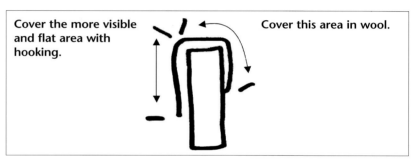

Cover the more visible and flat area with hooking.

Cover this area in wool.

Diagram of how to prepare the backing.

tern space. This is not difficult. You will know when you have the perfect layout. Tape the circles in place and trace them to create the pattern.

Preparing the Backing

Draw the outline to be hooked by laying the paper or fabric pattern "X" side up on the backing. Line up straight lines with the grain of the fabric then trace with a permanent marker. Draw the hooking design directly on the backing or draw it first on paper and transfer it with pattern tracing fabric, such as Red Dot.

If you are covering the curved areas with flat wool, mark that area on your pattern. Cut a piece of wool a bit larger than the area to be covered and stitch it in place. This can be done by hand or by using a sewing machine. I like to stitch it right sides together and then flip it back into place while I hook.

Diagram for shoulder bag handle. Start with a strip 3" wide. Fold in thirds and baste. Fold in thirds again and hem stitch.

This method makes a clean finish, securely attaches the wool, and I can hook right up to it. Leave the outer edges wild until you are ready to fit it to the handbag. More can be cut off later, but sewing on more at a later time is an unsightly bother.

Begin Hooking

This is a small piece of hooking that can be finished in a day or two. Try that new color scheme you were thinking about, match the colors in a favorite outfit, or use every color in the rainbow.

As you hook, compare the shape and size of the hooked piece with the item being covered, and adjust it as needed. Add or subtract a row or two so that the piece fits properly. Remember to allow extra space for the finishing if you are using a method that increases the size of the piece.

Handle

If you are covering an existing purse, you probably do not have to worry about the handle. But if you are using an unusual item, such as the pencil pouch I covered, you can use one of the many commercial handles available at craft and fabric shops. Be sure to purchase the handle first, before you begin the project. You can then adjust the colors or design to complement your chosen handle.

Use any strength features built into the item you are covering. Stitch through and around the hole reinforcement on the pencil pouch.

If a simple shoulder bag handle is preferred, you can make one out of a strip of wool. Tear a strip 3" wide from selvedge to selvedge. To determine the length, measure an existing handbag or safety pin the length of wool to the item being covered. Adjust it until it is just right.

Fold the piece lengthwise roughly into thirds and baste the loose edge in place. Fold again starting with the edge with the raw edge of the wool. If it is folded tightly, it will end up with a rounded shape. Carefully hemstitch the folded edge to the rest of the roll for the length of handle needed.

Finishing

Finish the hooked piece with your chosen method. As you work, carefully fit it to the item. This is the last chance to adjust the size so some extra time here will save headaches later. It is better to have the slip cover slightly larger than slightly smaller in most cases. Check to see if a slight overhang will interfere with the operation of closures, handles, etc.

Attaching the Slip Cover

Attach the handle securely to the item being covered. Remember that your hooking is only a slipcover. The item you are covering is where your valuables and weight will be.

Use a thick, strong thread such as buttonhole thread to securely attach the handle to the item being covered. Choose an area that will be covered by the hooking to hide the stitches. For the pencil pouch purse, I stitched the handle at each end of the backside of the top band. Later when I attached the hooked slipcover, it completely covered my messy stitching. If you have the reinforced holes of a pencil pouch, use their strength to securely attach the handle. Stitch over the edges of the hole to fasten the handle.

Now attach the slipcover to the face of the handbag using thread that matches the item. No fancy steps here. Just lay the hooking where you want it to end up and stitch it down. The item being covered is the actual

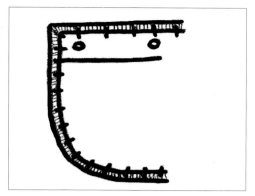

With the slipcover slightly larger than the pencil pouch, all that is needed are a few stitches around the edge to hold it in place.

handbag and you only need to make sure the hooking stays in place and does not flap around. Your valuables are safe because you are using a commercially constructed item to which you are simply attaching a slipcover. Keep your stitching neat. If the right color of thread or yarn is used, the attaching stitches will disappear. If there is a binding or edging on the purse flap, place your stitches in the ditch and they will completely disappear. When using a running stitch bury it between the loops. An added benefit is that if the cover is removed, the handbag fabric is not pierced with holes. I used this method on the small handbag and a simple hemstitch on the pencil pouch.

Cover undesirable sections of the item if needed. I covered the top band of the pencil pouch. The three holes used to place the pencil pouch in a three ring binder do not make sense on a purse. The pencil pouch often comes in colors that do not coordinate with your slipcover. Simply stitch a piece of

Designer's Tip

For a larger space to hook, consider a simple tote bag. These are sold very inexpensively at craft and fabric stores in many different sizes. Hook just one side, or hook them both.

A tote bag is also a great space to display seasonal hooked pieces. Choose a tote bag and determine the area for a smaller hooked piece. There is no need to cover the entire area. Then hook several pieces all the same size using different designs. Attach sew-on Velcro to the tote bag and to the back of your hooked piece. Cover the length of all four sides for the most secure attachment. Attach more Velcro to your extra pieces. Be sure to use the correct side, hook or loop. If you are unsure, try to attach a piece of Velcro to the tote bag's Velcro. If it does not lock on, you are using the wrong piece. Retest with the other side. Attach this to your hooked piece. Now the image on your bag can be changed as often as you like in seconds.

wool over the offending area so you have a completely coordinated look.

You are Done!

Fill your handbag with all your favorite things and wear it proudly. Be aware that fellow rug hookers are inclined to grab your purse for a closer look at any time. ●

ARTIST: CINDI GAY

As a child Cindi grew up with weekly art lessons at the Toledo Museum of Art, where her chosen medium was watercolor. While painting was Cindi's main expression of creativity, she still felt that something was missing. In 2000, Cindi began hooking after watching a TV show about rug hooking. Her first teacher, Jule Marie Smith, inspired her imagination over a weekend, and June Mikoryak in Allen Park, Michigan helped refine her critical eye and technique while also giving Cindi instructions on how to teach. Cindi now teaches in her home, at rug hooking shops, and at workshops across the country. She still hooks monthly with a small group of women in Sylvania, Ohio. These women were her first contact in the rug hooking world and have been her teachers, cheerleaders, and friends. Cindi is a McGown certified teacher, a member of ATHA and the Michigan Rugg Artistes, a McGown guild in Dearborn, Michigan.

Big Fish

BY GAIL DUFRESNE

I have wanted to hook a big fish for years. When Jenny asked me to submit a design for her book I was thrilled and decided that now was my chance! I loved every minute of hooking this guy.

Hairy, bleached linen was used as my backing and most of the body of the fish was hooked in a #6-cut of wool except for the eyes and parts of the face, which were hooked in a #3-cut. The trout was hooked horizontally except for the outline, the eyes, and parts of the mouth and gills, and the background and border were hooked vertically in a #8-cut of wool.

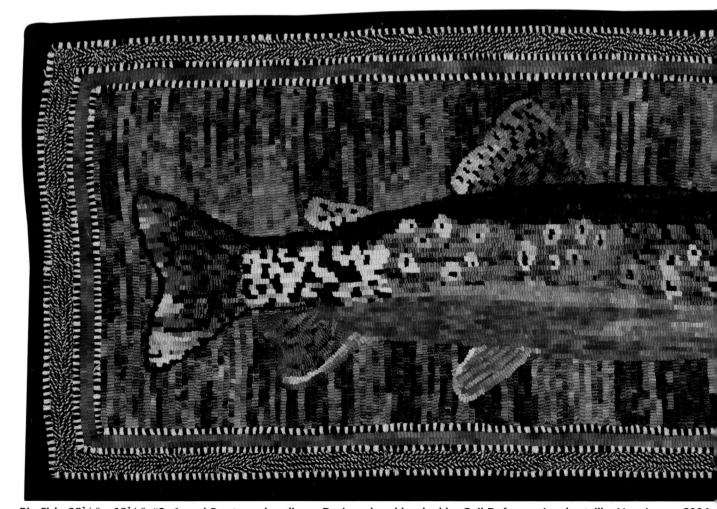

Big Fish, 38¹/₂" x 18¹/₂", #3, 6, and 8-cut wool on linen. Designed and hooked by Gail Dufresne, Lambertville, New Jersey, 2006.

Dye Formulas and Method of Dyeing

The dye formulas were kept very simple, using only four different PRO Chem wash-fast acid dyes: #119 Yellow, #351 Red, #490 Blue, #503 Brown, and #672 Black.

Regardless of the dye method used, your wool must be thoroughly soaked first. Wool should be soaked overnight but it is not necessary if a wetting agent (Jet Dri, Wetter Than Wet, or Synthropol) is used. Even if using one of these wetting agents, soak for at least an hour, although in a pinch I have waited for as little as five

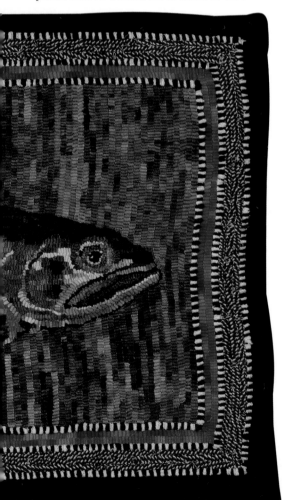

SPOT DYES::

Red Spot Dye
2 tsp PRO Chem #119 Yellow
2 tsp PRO Chem #351 Red

Medium Green Spot Dye
1 tsp PRO Chem #119 Yellow
$^1/_{64}$ tsp PRO Chem #351 Red
$^1/_{32}$ tsp PRO Chem #490 Blue
$^1/_{32}$ tsp PRO Chem #672 Black

Dissolve each dye separately into 2 to 4 cups of boiling water and work each color individually into $^1/_2$ yard of Dorr natural wool, repositioning the wool in the pan as you work.

HINT: After working the above dyes into the wool, dissolve another 1/2 teaspoon of PRO Chem #119 Yellow into 2 cups of boiling water and pour it over the top of the wool. Don't work it in. The wool will glow and look more "fishy," or iridescent.

Dark Green Spot Dye:
Spot $^1/_2$-yard Dorr 44 wool or any dark green wool with $^1/_2$-teaspoon PRO Chem #672 Black.

Dissolve the dye into 2 cups of boiling water. Pour half of it over the wool, working it in. Reposition the wool in the pan and pour the rest of the dye solution over the wool, working it in again.

Brown Spot Dye For Background
Spot $^1/_2$-yard Dorr natural with 1 tsp #503 Brown.
Spot $^1/_2$-yard Dorr natural with $^1/_2$ tsp #503 Brown.
Spot $^1/_2$-yard Dorr natural with $^1/_4$ tsp #503 Brown.

Transitional Painted Wool:
Scrunch a full yard of Dorr natural wool into a 2" x 13" x 18" pan, with the two selvedges at the 18" ends of the pan.

Dissolve 1 teaspoon of PRO Chem #119 Yellow into 2 to 4 cups of boiling water and work the yellow into the entire piece of wool, repositioning the wool to ensure full coverage.

Dissolve $^1/_{16}$ teaspoon of PRO Chem #351 Red into 2 cups of boiling water. Work most of the dye solution into the bottom half of the wool and then move up the long side of the pan, working in the dye. Blend some into the yellow area to soften the yellow a bit.

minutes and the wetting agents had pretty thoroughly soaked through the wool.

Scrunch an entire yard of wool into a pan that is 2" deep, 13" wide and 18" long. If dyeing less than a yard of wool, use a smaller pan so that the wool is really tightly scrunched. This is how to get those great peaks and valleys of mottled color. The wool is repositioned as the dye is worked in to ensure full coverage. I like to use my (gloved) hands to work the dye into the wool, but use your own weapon of choice: spoon, potato masher, whatever.

Please note that it is standard practice to give dye formulas using $1/2$ yard of wool, which is how I wrote most of mine unless a different amount of wool is specifically indicated. If you choose to dye a yard at a time you will need to double some of my dye formulas.

After dyeing the wool, spread 1 teaspoon of citric acid or $1/3$ cup vinegar around the wool, at the sides of the pan. There should be at least a $1/2$" of water in the pan; enough so that the wool will not burn when steaming or baking. Cover the pan with aluminum foil and steam for at least 20 minutes on top of the stove at medium heat or bake in the oven at 300° for one hour. After the wool has completely cooled in the pan, machine-wash it in cold water, using no soap, and dry it in the dryer with a towel and a fabric softener sheet.

Hooking the Fish

The fish was hooked first using the following amounts of wool:

Red spot dye: $3/16$ yard
Medium green spot dye: $3/16$ yard
Dark green spot dye: $1/8$ yard
Brown background spot dye: $1/16$ yard
Transitional wool: $1/8$ yard

I tend to hook low and if you do, too, you may want to allow for more wool. First the eye was hooked in a #3 cut of wool, using the dark green spot and some of the yellow to red dip-dye. Don't forget the white highlight. The only curved lines in the fish are the outline, the eyes, the mouth, and two lines to set the gills. The rest of the fish was hooked horizontally in a #6 cut. The wool was clipped frequently to make color changes, especially around the dark spots. The brown background spot dye was used in the gills area and on the front fin.

Beading

After the fish was hooked, the outline between the background and the border was hooked with the dark green spot dye and as-is (not overdyed) white wool, using a technique called beading.

There is no way to avoid creating a slight twist in the wool on the back of your work, as you need to bring one wool around the other.

Holding two cut strips of wool, one the dark green spot dye and one the undyed white, between your thumb and forefinger, bring both ends up through the backing, exactly as you would with a single strip. Make a loop with one of the strips, either color. Bring the other color around the first color with your hook and make a second loop. Alternate colors.

There is no way to avoid creating a slight twist in the wool on the back of your work, as you need to bring one wool around the other. You may not want to use this technique on floor rugs as the twisted wool might wear faster than the rest of the rug. Allow for $3/32$ yards of wool, half dark green spot dye and half white.

Hooking the Background

The background was hooked vertically using $3/4$ yard of three different values of wool spot dyed with PRO Chem #503 Brown. Again, I hook low—you may need more. I cut the wool and mixed it up, hooking it randomly for most of the background. I chose the proper value of wool I used next to the fish to make sure that all of the fish stood out prominently, using darker values of background wool next to lighter areas of the fish and vice versa.

Hooking the Border

There are nine lines in the border, after the beaded line separating the background from the border. Allow for at least $3/32$-yard wool per borderline. The borderlines were hooked using the following:
- Two lines of the red spot dye
- One line of beading using the dark green spot dye and as-is (undyed) white wool

Designer's Tip: Borders

Usually, I like some sort of border on my rug to complete it and "settle it down," even if it is only a row or two of hooking. Generally, I like to pull out the darkest and/or dullest colors used in the rug. I rarely introduce a color that has not already been used in the inner design. As always, there are exceptions to every rule and my own "rules" have been broken on more than one occasion.

I originally intended to have about a 9" border with, among other things, two rows of dark green and white squares. After nine rows (or 2^1/$_2$") I stopped, because the time to complete this project ran out, and I also liked the look! What is interesting is that, as a general rule, I find designs that are twice as long as they are wide, pleasing, and this is almost exactly the ratio of this design. The beaded line of very dark, almost black, dark green spot dye mixed with the stark white wool is a real eye popper. The as-is dark brown tweed seems to shimmer and move and makes me a little dizzy when I stare at it. I like that! It also reminds me a little of fish bones. It is daring and dramatic and yet it doesn't detract from the fish.

> *I like some sort of border on my rug to complete it and "settle it down," even if it is only a row or two of hooking.*

- Three lines of a dark brown and white as-is tweed
- One line of beading using the dark green spot dye and as-is (undyed) white wool
- Two lines of the dark green spot dye

Steaming

Lay a blanket or towel on a hard surface. Don't steam on a wooden surface such as a hardwood floor as moisture may damage it. Place the rug, wrong side up, on top of the blanket or towel. Completely soak another towel and wring it out slightly. Place the towel over the rug. Using a medium to high steam setting, place the iron on the wet towel for a few seconds, and then lift the iron to another spot on the wet towel. Continue this process until the entire rug has been steamed. **No pressure is needed on the iron.** Turn the rug over and repeat this process. Let the rug dry thoroughly. Repeat the entire process if the rug still does not lay flat. I usually steam my rug before and after it is finished.

Finishing

I prefer to use wool to finish my rugs rather than whipping and as many of you know my husband does it for me! I like the look of using the same wool that was hooked into the border for the binding. The dark green spot dyed wool was used, which was also the wool used in the last two border lines.

Before hooking the last few rows, hand or machine-sew about a 3" strip of the same wool used for the border to the edge of the rug. Hook up to the wool strip. Cording is optional, but if used, place the cord on the wrong side of the rug and fold the backing over the cord. Baste it into place. If cording is not used, consider leaving a narrow strip of the wool showing on the front side of the rug. Hand-sew the edge to the back of the rug. ●

ARTIST: GAIL DUFRESNE

Gail Dufresne has been hooking since August 1984. Her mother, Doris LaPlante, hooked for 38 years and her sister, Yvonne Wood, has hooked for over 40. She is a member of the editorial board for Rug Hooking *magazine, where she regularly contributes articles. Her rugs have been finalists in* A Celebration of Hand-Hooked Rugs VII, VIII, IX, XII and XIII, *and she was a participant in Linda Rae Coughlin's "Art" of Playing Cards project, where she designed and hooked the Ace of Hearts. Gail's rugs have been featured in exhibits at the Wadsworth Athenaeum in Hartford, Connecticut and at the Textile Center of Minnesota. In 2004 she was the featured teacher and artist at Sauder Village. Gail is a McGown certified teacher and has been teaching since 1999. She also teaches at camps and private workshops around the United States and Canada since April 2000.*

Gram's Pocket Purse

BY KIM DUBAY

For years, I have been hooking projects as part of a series I like to call my "Hooked Heirlooms." It started when my grandparent's house needed to be cleaned out and sold. Many odds and ends came into my possession. To me, they were treasures, not to be sold or given away outside of the family, but what would I do with it all? Or, better yet, how would I display them if I wanted to do so? My mother's baby clothes, an old suitcase, wool shirts, and a wooden barrel stave were just some of what was found. These were pieces of history—family history—that needed to be preserved.

WHAT YOU NEED:

- Wool pocket (cut away from the shirt)
- Linen (or desired backing) 30" x 20"
- Wide belt or leather strap
- Fat quarter yard of cotton fabric
- Fabric covered button kit
- Cardboard $7^1/2$" x $3^1/2$"
- Button and carpet thread
- Hooking supplies
- Wool (amounts to follow)
- Wool roving
- Needle felting needles
- Foam
- Elmer's glue
- Fray Check (optional)
- Pattern transfer material i.e. Red Dot Tracer (optional)
- Sharpie marker

Gram's Pocket Purse, 11" x 22", #6 cut wool on linen. Designed and hooked by Kim Dubay, No. Yarmouth, Maine, 2005.

WOOL AMOUNTS:

- Scraps for flowers, leaves and stems, and for flower on button

- 29" x 12" mock paisley wool

- $\frac{1}{3}$ yard sage green wool plus 2" x 5$\frac{1}{2}$" wool tabs

- 5" square mustard wool for button

Please Note: These wool amounts are based on the sample purse made. The amounts could differ according to the size of your pocket, hooking style, width of wool, and cut of strip used. (The sample was hooked in a #6 cut).

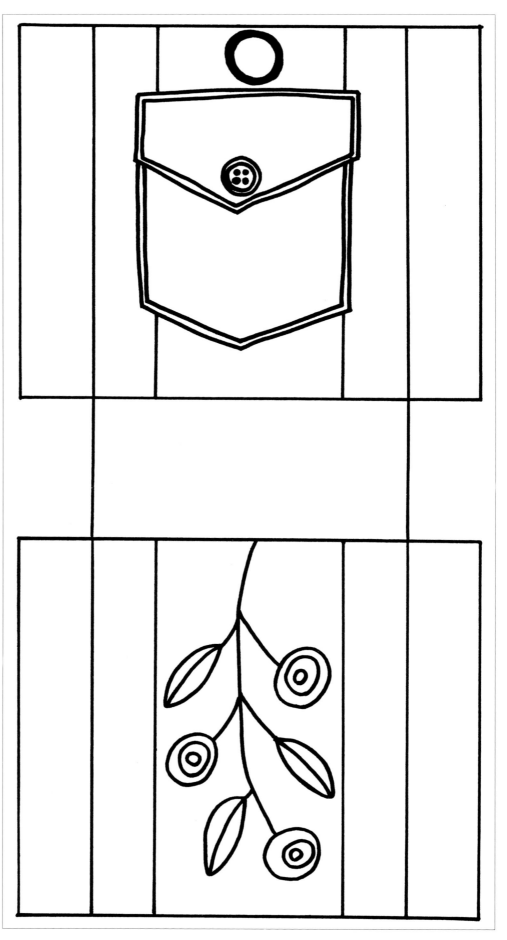

My grandparents always marveled at some of the things I created many times using nothing more than trash. In their honor, I felt I needed to create something of value from the things they no longer had any use for. *Gram's Pocket Purse* is the last in this series.

First Step
Maybe you already have a wool shirt from a family member that you would like to commemorate, making it into a hooked work of art. If not, wool shirts can be found at rummage sales, thrift shops, or yard sales. Once you have a shirt, your story can begin.

The first step is to embellish the wool pocket before attaching it to the pattern. I had many ideas as how to decorate my pocket. My grandmother always tended flower gardens so I thought a flower design would remind me of her. Since the pattern had flowers on the backside, I decided to continue that theme on the front.

The flowers could be made by using buttons, then embroidering the leaves and stems. Or the flowers could be appliquéd with a wool circle attached by using a blanket stitch and any other embroidery stitches that would replicate flowers, i.e. the stem stitch, lazy daisy stitch, etc.

My choice was to try needle felting the flowers onto the pocket. This technique uses a special, long, barbed needle and wool roving. A piece of foam is needed inside the pocket so that the needle doesn't come through to the back layer of the pocket. The wool roving is laid onto the surface of the pocket in small amounts, held by your finger and is agitated by inserting the needle, straight up and down, through the roving, the pocket and then through the foam. It is the heat and friction that adheres the wool fibers together. This action is done quickly so be sure to keep your fingers away from the needle. If you look inside the pocket, between the front and the foam, you should see the wool fibers coming through. That will assure you that the wool roving has attached itself to the wool pocket. Continue to lay the roving on top of itself until it is to your lik-

ing. Colors can be added on top of one another to achieve the desired look.

Back view of *Gram's Pocket Purse* by Kim Dubay

The Pattern
The pattern (shown) needs to be enlarged at the local copy center. Ask them to print it out to a finished size of 11" x 22". When transferring the pattern from paper to backing, I recommend measuring the placement of all the straight lines and that they be drawn with a lead pencil drug along the grooves of the weave then traced over with a permanent Sharpie marker. The flowers can be drawn by using either Red Dot tracer paper or taping your paper pattern to a glass window or a light box, then centering the backing over it to trace. **NOTE: *The pocket shown is for placement only. It is not to be drawn onto the backing.***

Check the placement of the pocket on the pattern's diagram making sure that the bottom of the pocket is toward the bottom of the purse. Pin the finished pocket onto the pattern. This is to be hand-sewn using your choice of thread; then blanket-stitch it into place. I used an ecru-colored button and carpet thread that matched closely to my pocket color. An alternate technique is to use the blind stitch so that the stitches don't show.

At this point, I would do a zigzag-stitch row away from the pattern's outside edge. This is easier to do now before the hooking begins. This row will keep the backing from fraying into the hooked design once the excess is cut away for finishing. A serger can be used for this step but that would be done after the hooking is complete.

The Hooking

The hooking can be done in a #6, #7, or a #8 cut strip. Mine was done in a #6. I would first hook the bottom of the purse. An important note: Place the first hooked row of each area on the inside of the drawn line, not on it, to insure a correct fit when sewing the purse together. Make sure that you stay within the same outline row of the backing so that the purse stays square.

After the bottom of the purse is hooked, start on the back with the flowers, leaves, and stems. Fill in the background around them, then onto the side panels. When hooking the panels beside the flower center, follow the contour for two rows then fill in with vertical rows. Do this for all the panels and flaps on both sides of the purse. By following these contours, the purse will naturally fold on the lines that were drawn and make the purse stand like a box.

Turn the pattern over and hook the center panel above and below the pocket. Then move to the panel and flap on either side, hooking the two contour rows then the vertical rows to fill.

Finishing

When the purse is completely hooked, use a damp cloth or towel to press from the backside using the wool setting and a no steam iron. Do not press from the front because of the shirt pocket and embellishments. Let the purse air-dry.

Now cut beside the zigzag row and remove the excess backing. (If using the serger, it is done at this point). With scissors, cut a diagonal slit into each corner of the bottom of the purse and secure it with Fray Check or Elmer's glue. Once these areas are dry, use a hot iron to press the seam allowance to the backside of the purse all the way around.

Cut two tabs from the sage green wool used, 2"x 5$\frac{1}{2}$". Fold in thirds the long way and stitch closed with matching thread. Press with an iron to flatten. Set aside.

The Belt Handle

To make the belt handle, put it together at the longest length and fold it in half with the buckle closest to one of the folds but leaving enough space for a loop. Put an elastic band at each end where a grommet would be and secure. I took my belt to a local shoe repairman and it took him five minutes and a nominal fee to make the holes and insert the grommets.

Next, lay the purse flat, wrong side up on a table. Measure the overall length and width and add $\frac{1}{2}$" to each measurement. This is the size of the lining. Cut out the lining fabric and press with a hot iron a seam allowance to the wrong side all the way around. Now pin all four sides of the lining to the hooked purse, wrong sides together. Leave the "U" shaped areas unpinned where the bottom of the purse is. Turn the purse over, the right side facing you. Using scissors cut away the excess fabric leaving a seam allowance on all three sides. Then cut a slit diagonally into each corner (like you did on the backing) so that the lining fabric will turn under. No need to press these seams, just crease with the fingers and pin in place.

At the center of the back flower panel, pin and sew a strip of wool $\frac{1}{4}$" x 7" folded in half for the loop closure. Insert the strip ends below the edge between the lining fabric and the hooked purse. Be sure that the stitches don't show through onto the hooked side.

The hooked button was made by hooking through a piece of wool then making the button according to the enclosed instructions. Sew the button now centered on the front above the pocket. Unpin the lining so that you can stitch this without it showing on the inside of the purse.

With matching thread, blind stitch by hand around the entire purse, sewing the lining to the edge of the backing. Try to cover

If you are lucky enough to have objects from your family you'd like to preserve, start with those. If not, hunt around antique shops or flea markets for cast-off oddities that will become your treasures.

all of the backing by gently pulling on the lining fabric as you sew. When you get near the top on both front and back, insert the wool tabs you made earlier into the belt loops (sewn side of the tab folded on the inside). Pin the tab ends into place between the lining and the hooked layer, from each side seam and down into the lining. Sew back and forth three times to secure each tab. Continue sewing the lining until completed.

After the lining is in place, it's time to sew the side seams. Butt the side flap panels against the short side of the bottom, one at a time, and sew with a light-colored button and carpet thread. Try pinning these into place or what I did was just hold the flap and bottom edge together as you sew. I found the ladder stitch works best for this. Sew your stitches into the backing so that the hooked rows meet. This makes it virtually impossible to see the seam or any of the backing. After both the bottom seams are sewn, go up the side seam. Repeat for the second side.

Cut a piece of cardboard $7^1/2$" x $3^1/2$" for the bottom of the purse. Taking your leftover lining fabric, cover both sides and glue with Elmer's. This will be inserted inside the bottom to help it stand on its own.

The last step in doing my "Hooked Heirlooms" is to include a story with each piece. Someday, when my son finds them, he will be able to read about the when, where, and why of what I did. Normally, I handwrite and laminate the stories, then I find a way to attach them. This time I did a special "Artist Trading Card" with pictures of my grandmother and I, and the story hand-stamped on the back. It goes as follows: "Last in my heirloom series, my grandmother loves gardening and I love my handbags. Made by using a wool shirt pocket of hers and a belt of mine." It is the size of a playing card ($2^1/2$"x$3^1/2$"), so it fits perfectly into the shirt pocket for safekeeping.

I hope this project helps you use found objects with your hooking for telling family stories. We don't have to limit ourselves to two-dimensional work. Start looking at everything around you with fresh, new eyes and you'll be surprised at what you'll discover. Use your imagination to come up with unique and clever designs for ordinary objects. Your kids will be left with great memories, and you'll have so much fun doing it! ●

ARTIST: KIM DUBAY

A Maine native, Kim has been active in the arts from an early age. Proficient in fiber art, Kim has been designing and producing hooked rugs and supplies since 1993 under the name of Primitive Pastimes. Her studio in North Yarmouth, Maine is a fun-filled space full of artistic surprises. Kim's work has been featured in fiber art publications including several Rug Hooking *magazine issues and their* Basic Rug Hooking *book along with last year's new book* Hooked Rugs Today *by Amy Oxford. She has also contributed hooked rugs to such projects as the Green Mountain Rug Hooking Guild's Circus Train; the Vermont Vignette collection; and Linda Rae Coughlin's "Art" Rugs-The Art of Playing Cards. She has taught in her hometown, along with three years at the Green Mountain Rug Hooking Guild's annual workshop and is currently at Artascope Studios in the Art Night Out program. Gram's Pocket Purse pattern is available through: Kim Dubay/Primitive Pastimes, 410 Walnut Hill Road, North Yarmouth, Maine 04097, (207) 829-3725, KimDubay410@aol.com, or www.primitivepastimes.net.*

Geometric Pillow

BY SALLY KORTE AND ALICE STREBEL

The design for this pillow is bold, bright, funky, and innovative—evident in the highly contrasting colors and the clean-lined geometric shapes. The "funkiness" is also in plain sight with the choice of oversized covered buttons that have been hooked and put to use closing the band of the pillow cover. The innovative aspect of the design is not so obvious and requires an introduction. The red and gold fabric that the design is hooked into is ordinary linen foundation fabric that has been hand-dyed.

WHAT YOU NEED:

- Linen rug hooking foundation fabric: A 20" x 25" piece to dye for the gold areas and a 27" x 36" piece to dye for the red areas

- Two colors of PRO Chem's dyes for cotton

- PRO Chem dye activator

- Black, gold, and red wool

- Two 10" x 19" pieces of black wool for the band on the pillow

- Three 2¹/₂" covered buttons (the kind with the teeth)

- Two 20" x 22" piece of fabric for the pillow form

- Stuffing for the pillow

- A chalk pencil

- A primitive hook

The concept of dyeing wonderful colors of foundation fabric creates a whole new wonderland of possibilities for hooking projects. Just think of the things you could make by hooking only the motifs and leaving the hand-dyed linen as the backdrop of the design.

Dying the Linen

The first step is to stabilize the linen by sewing along any raw edges to prevent raveling. Take the sizing out of the fabric by washing and drying the linen.

Please familiarize yourself with the manufacturers' directions for using the dye. Their directions for dyeing are based on the use and weight of cotton. The linen fabric weighs much more than the cotton for the same measurement of fabric and requires three to four times their recommendations for both the dye and the dye activator to successfully create a rich deep color.

Hooking and Construction

Sew ¹/₂" seams throughout this project.

1. First prepare the front of the pillow cover that is constructed of nine squares of dyed linen sewn together. With a chalk pencil mark six 7" squares on the red linen and three 7" squares on the gold linen. The squares need to be separated from each other by at least a ¹/₂". In order to prevent rampant fraying when the linen is cut into pieces sew on all of the marked lines. Be careful not to stretch the linen as you sew. Next cut out all the squares **right beside** and outside the sewn lines.

2. Referring to the diagram for color placement sew all the squares together. Press the seams open.

3. The hooking design comes to within a ¹/₂" of the edge of the linen fabric. In order to be able to hook this close to the edges enlarge the piece by cutting the "unwanted" fabric into four strips and baste them with ¹/₂" seams around the outside edges of the linen.

4. Next mark the hooking design on the linen backing with the chalk pencil. Mark the six triangles on the red squares and the three stars on the gold squares.

5. Cut the wool for hooking in ¹/₄" strips (#8-cut). First hook the triangles. Hook right up against the seam lines. First outline only the "V" part of the triangles in red. Next hook the first row at the base of the triangles (that are up against the seams) in black. Continue on to fill in the triangles alternating rows of black and gold. Hook the stars all in black. Set aside.

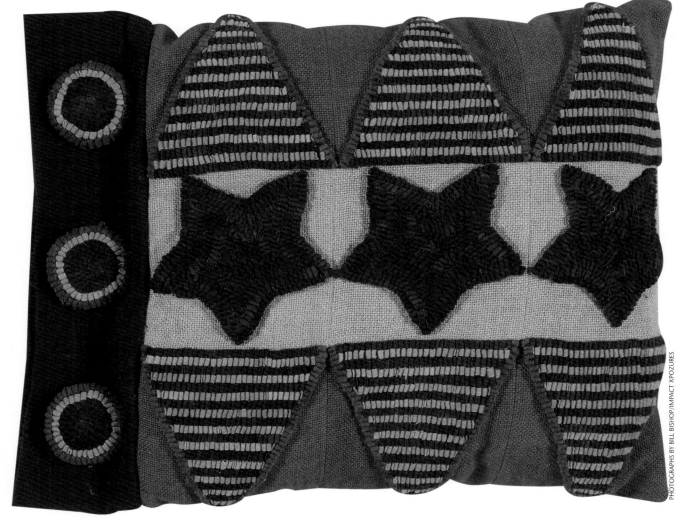

Geometric Pillow, 22¹/₂" x 18", #8-cut wool on linen. Designed and hooked by Kindred Spirits, Kettering, Ohio, 2005.

6. The next step is to prepare the back of the pillow cover. The back is constructed of three rows of the hand-dyed linen. The center row is gold with a row of red on each side. See diagram. Trace two 7" x 19" rectangles on the red linen and one rectangle on the gold linen. Sew on the traced linen then cut them out the rectangles just as you did for the front of the pillow cover. Sew the three strips together.

7. Pin together the front and back of the pillow cover with right sides facing and matching all the seams. Sew together three sides of pillow cover leaving one end next to a star open. Turn right side out and press.

8. The next step is to attach the black band. First place the two pieces of black wool right sides together and sew

the two 10" side seams creating a tube. Fold the tube in half and press so now the band is 5" wide. Place the unfinished end of the pillow inside the black band matching the side seams and the straight raw edges even. Sew the band onto the pillow cover. Turn right side out and press.

9. Continue on to hook the three covered buttons. Use the red hand-dyed linen as the foundation fabric. There is probably not enough red linen left to fit in your frame, therefore some trouble shooting suggestions include— using a smaller hoop; adding fabric strips to enlarge the size; or just catching two or three sides of the fabric you have on the frame and toughing it out.

10. Use the circle for the back of the covered button as a template. Trace

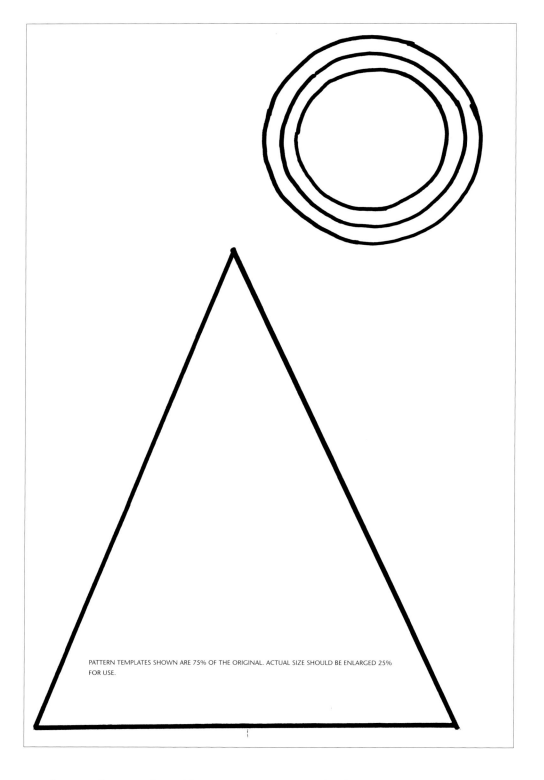

PATTERN TEMPLATES SHOWN ARE 75% OF THE ORIGINAL. ACTUAL SIZE SHOULD BE ENLARGED 25% FOR USE.

three circles onto the red linen at least 1$^1/_2$" apart. Hook the outer circle in red, next hook one row of gold, and then fill in with the black.

11. After the hooking is done assemble the hooked buttons according to the package directions. Attach buttons to the inside black band of the pillow equidistance apart from each other.

12. Make the three buttons holes on the front band of the pillow cover centered on the 4$^1/_2$" width and equidistance apart from each other.

13. Almost done now. The last step is to make the stuffed pillow. Place the two pieces of fabric for the pillow right sides together. Sew all the way around leaving an opening along one edge.

Turn right side out through the opening. Stuff the pillow keeping it fairly flat like the pillows for a bed. Insert buttons through the button-holes to close. ●

Just think of the things you could make by hooking only the motifs and leaving the hand-dyed linen as the backdrop of the design.

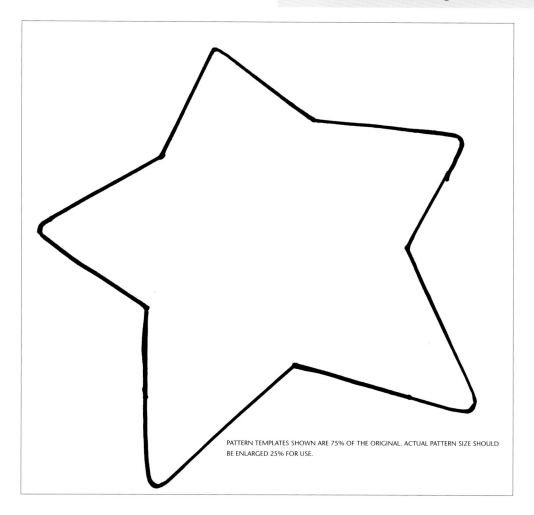

PATTERN TEMPLATES SHOWN ARE 75% OF THE ORIGINAL. ACTUAL PATTERN SIZE SHOULD BE ENLARGED 25% FOR USE.

ARTISTS: SALLY KORTE AND ALICE STREBEL

Sally Korte and Alice Strebel are indeed kindred spirits. Sharing the same joy found in expressing themselves through their creations, and an appreciation of all things, inspired them to begin a business, Kindred Spirits, formed in 1986 when the two friends began publishing patterns and books. Sally and Alice are involved in lecturing and teaching nationally as well as internationally and they like to consider themselves motivational speakers on the topic of personal creativity.

Log Cabin Collection

BY SUSAN FELLER, RUCKMAN MILL FARM

Do you have a great farm table in your dining room just waiting to be decorated? This project was conceived to reward the crafts person with easy "modules," which can be completed in a short time frame. Once the color planning and design choices are completed, each element is portable with a flexible concept also. Shown are the placemats, but by attaching other elements, a table runner, floor rug, or great accent pillows are possible.

WHAT YOU NEED FOR PLACEMATS:

(other projects will vary)

- Foundation material of choice (monk's cloth, rug warp, linen) cut into six pieces 20" x 24".

- Wool in $1/4$ yard units—24 to 30 comprised of six colors, 4 or 5 pieces each in a variety of textures and values.

- Binding material of choice. (I suggest light and dark to enhance design.)

Drawing the Patterns

The set of patterns includes a log cabin, tree, running deer, fox, chunky lion, and sheep. Consider how you want the overall collection to be presented before drawing the patterns. One animal could be flipped to create a set facing its mate, or all could "walk" around in single file. The border unites the collection with the $1^3/4$" wide strips butting to each other as they close around the edges. Note the consistency in position, especially if you are connecting modules for a table runner or rug.

Color Planning

Now to the exciting and tricky section; remember there are six patterns—six bars in the border, six inner backgrounds, and six images. That is why we suggest you select six colors! In the selection of those colors it is very important to include a variety of textures, solids, and several values. Each will come in handy as you plan the colors for each unit. Divide your colors into piles and code each with a letter or number for identification on a chart or the patterns. I actu- ally cut a strip of each and stapled them to a sheet for each pattern, labeling the color and part of the design to which they corre- sponded.

First decide which color will be the primary for the characters and select one family for each. As you can see in the examples there are crossovers but one color is dominant. Now code the back- grounds. I used solids for the background, intermingling some different values where needed for interest. This way the designs are the focus. Take care to consider con- trast. When there was not enough value difference, I hooked in an outline of #5- cut wool or even pulled up a line of yarn as on the fox.

Code the border strips by taking one color family, using all the choices at least once on a different strip per pattern. It is not as simple as following the same rou- tine with each color moving on to the next strip because sometimes the back- ground color will be the strip next to it also. You could complicate matters and create a log cabin in half-dark and half- light values. Having a variety of values is essential.

Set of six designs for 12" x 16" mats with Log Cabin Quilt Border, #5, 6, and 8-cut wool on monk's cloth. Designed by Susan Feller, Augusta, West Virginia. Hooked by Susan Feller; Rosemary Glennon, Califon, New Jersey; and Linda Ratliff, Romney, West Virginia, 2005.

The color families used for the samples are orange, yellow, red, green, purple, and neutrals. I used two yarns to whip the edges—dark antique black and light moss green. If the borders had been planned in half-dark and half-light the whipping could have finished them off with contrasting or similar values for each half. These details will make your project unique.

Details on Patterns

For the log cabin there are several things to consider—whether there is someone home; are the lights on in both windows; are the curtains pulled or is just a candle burning? Note the contrasting line of chinking between the top log and roof to define each.

The tree can be in fall foliage, bare for winter, or in early spring colors. Note the bit of interest in the trunk using a variegated

PATTERN COPYRIGHT © SUSAN FELLER, 2005. THE PATTERN IS FOR PERSONAL USE ONLY, THE PATTERN MAY NOT BE DUPLICATED FOR MASS USE OR SOLD. NOR MAY RUGS MADE FROM THIS PATTERN BE SOLD. ACTUAL PATTERN SIZE SHOULD BE ENLARGED TO 12" X 16" FOR USE.

wool strip. Because of contrast problems the entire tree was outlined to enhance the design.

The lion needs outline accents of #5 cut with a body in a #8 or #6. The sheep could use some outlining to define the head section.

Note that the fox and deer are running and the pair of legs farthest away from us should be hooked in a darker value; same with the sheep.

Other Projects

The exciting part of this project is its potential. Using the unifying border design, the patterns can be repeated or combined endlessly.

A table runner could comprise three or more designs 16" wide by increments of 12". One more rectangle design could be made by continuing the log cabin strips into the center, remembering to intersect each length with the next side as on the outside

First decide which color will be the primary for the characters and select one family for each.

edges. This mat could serve as a potholder, teapot rest, or design element in the runner.

A rug for the floor could be made running two rows side by side. This would make a 32" x 72" rug, if you alternated with the log cabin filler mat and had 12 sections. Hook one row of contrasting color in between each block and use the same color to whip the edge.

The 12" x 16" size is perfect as an accent pillow. Using a pillow form 2" larger than your design will create a plump accessory. Whip the entire mat then cut a complimenting piece of fabric (textured wool is a great surprise) 14" x 18". Turn the fabric edges 1" on each side and press flat, pin with wrong sides together, and hand stitch the backer through the rug edge at the base of whipping. Stitch three sides, then insert the pillow form, pin, and stitch it closed. With this technique your welted edge around the mat completes the pillow look without any other upholstery construction.

Level of Skill

This project would be suitable for beginners. The straight hooking and lessons in color planning would build confidence and the small size of each is rewarding. Rosemary Glennon, age 16, hooked the sheep mat and this was her second project.

Intermediate hookers will also enjoy hooking these mats by approaching the color planning and more intricate designs as challenges. Linda Ratliff has hooked since 1999 and recently has become aware

> *Consider a group project for a couple of meetings; each member contributing wool and color planning ideas.*

of values and contrast in design. She hooked the log cabin and fox. Linda hooks primarily with a #6 and didn't hook the border in vertical rows but created a curving design and filled the spaces.

Consider a group project for a couple of meetings; each member contributing wool and color planning ideas. Bring the mats together when finished for a potluck dinner party.

Availability of Patterns

The patterns can be ordered from *Ruckman Mill Farm, PO Box 409, Augusta, WV 26704*; telephone (304) 496-8073, drawn as a set (spaced as if you are hooking each separately) on monk's cloth for $100 or on linen for $135. Call it the "Log Cabin Collection" when ordering. Individual designs, table runner, or rug are included in our pattern catalog available for $5. For more information see Susan's web site at *www.ruckmanmillfarm.com.* ●

ARTIST: SUSAN FELLER

The recycling aspect of rug hooking, its ties to colonial life, and the tactile excitement of wools, all added up to a new world for Susan in 1994. A one-hour lesson and many back issues of Rug Hooking *magazine specifically helped push her creativity. As president for 2006–2009 pf TIGHR (the International Guild of Handhooked Rugmakers, www.tighr.org), Susan wll be meeting fiber artists around the world. Information on her rug pattern line, hand-dyed wools, and teaching schedule are available through Ruckman Mill Farm, at www.ruckmanmillfarm.com. Susan lives with her partner in their log home in Augusta, West Virginia.*

Fantasy Garden Tote

BY SUSAN QUICKSALL

Whimsical, yet stylish, Fantasy Garden Tote is not only fun to hook but may become one of your favorite fashion accessories for your fall and winter wardrobe. The front of the tote features a spray of primitive posies and leaves, hooked in shades of coral, red, gold, teal, and greens. More flowers and vines continue onto the backside of the tote along with a colorful bird. The hooked bottom of the tote is yet another posy and leaf pattern, all set on a dark "black-of-many-colors" background which let the flower colors dance in their own fantasy garden.

Fantasy Garden Tote Bag, 9" H x 13^1/$_2$" W x 4^1/$_2$" D, #6 and #7-cut wool on linen. Designed and hooked by Susan Quicksall, Oglesby, Texas, 2005.

Fantasy Garden Tote consists of three hooked pieces—a front, a back, and a bottom. Short wool-covered cord handles, or longer shoulder straps, and a pocketed wool lining complete this easy-to-carry (and find everything) tote. It can be assembled completely by hand if necessary and whipped together easily. It's ready for the hard wear most totes get; its durability due to the application of a paint-on rug backing onto the backside of the hooked area before the lining is attached. Of course, as purists, we rug hookers wouldn't dream of "painting" rug backing on our soon-to-be-heirloom rugs. But, to keep a hooked strip (that finally-perfect flower center or bird beak) securely in place when doing battle with car keys, hooks, and other "snaggers" lurking in our tote, it has an advantage worth considering. In addition, it adds needed stability to this bucket-style tote.

Enlarging and Transferring the Pattern

Enlarge the three-piece pattern art **as one piece** so that the pieces seam together precisely and the bottom fits on easily. **I recommend not hooking the pieces on separate pieces of backing.** So whether you choose to enlarge the pattern by hand on grid lines or take it to the local print/copy store, enlarge the entire pattern as a whole. *Fantasy Garden Tote* needs to be enlarged so that the measurements of the tote front are: across the top $13^1/4$"; height 9"; and across the bottom $10^1/4$". The remaining back and base will enlarge accordingly.

I use Scottish linen exclusively in my pattern designs, but whatever you choose consider one that does not stretch or

WHAT YOU NEED:

WOOL NEEDED

Fantasy Garden Tote is a great project to use leftover scraps or cut strips. I hooked using a #7-cut strip with some #6-cuts where needed. The colors used were some of the 44 dye formulas from Holly Hill Designs' dye book *Mellow Colors for Rug Hooking*, available from this author. You may also choose to use the accompanying photos of formula swatches to select similar hues and values from your own wool stash. Following are approximate amounts of wool colors needed for hooking as well as materials needed for the finishing of your tote.

- **Background:** $1/2$-yard total of assorted darks such as Stencil Brown, Compost, Licorice, Chimney Soot, and Eggplant dyed over various textures and solids. Add some very dark green and navy too.

- **Fan Flower, Round Flowers, Bird:** $1/8$-yard total of coral such as Hearth Stone in various values dyed over Dorr Natural, #42 or oatmeal, and herringbone.

- **Leaves:** $1/4$-yard total of assorted sage, olive, and greens such as: Potting Shed Green, Lily Pond, and Olive Flora dyed over Dorr Oatmeal, #42 and light textures.

- **Stems, Tulip Flower, Bird:** $1/8$-yard total of assorted brown-golds such as Indian Moon Gold, Marmalade, and Firefly dyed over Dorr's Natural, #46, camel glen plaid.

- **Star Flowers, Leaves, Flower Centers:** $1/4$-yard total of various values of teal such as Cat Hollow and Majolica Green dyed over natural, herringbone, light textures.

- **Bird Wing, Flower Centers:** $1/8$-yard total of red such as Holly Hill Red dyed over Dorr Natural, oatmeal, and camel herringbone.

- **Light Beige-Gold Outlines, Leaves:** $1/8$-yard total of light beige-golds such as Beeswax and Aged Linen dyed over light camel herringbone, oatmeal, and natural.

- **Accent Colors for Flower Centers, Stems, and Bird:** Accent colors such as Horse Apples, Bittersweet, and Tin Bin Blue dyed over oatmeal or taupe textures.

FINISHING MATERIALS NEEDED

- **Lining and Handle Fabric:** $1/2$-yard hand-dyed or as-is wool plaid or textures. A lighter weight wool works best for lining.

- **Tub of MCG Textiles brand rug backing** (available at national chain hobby stores)

- **Paint brush:** $1/2$" wide, economy

- **Pillow cording for handles:** 1 yard of "Jumbo"($1/2$"diameter), polyester, for short handles. (1 $1/2$ yard for shoulder straps).

- **Pillow cording for top edge:** 1 yard of "narrow" ($3/16$" diameter), polyester, for top edge to be over-whipped with wool strips or yarn.

- **Thread:** heavy-duty (button/craft) sewing thread

Fantasy Garden Tote back view. Designed and hooked by Susan Quicksall, 2005.

I use Scottish linen exclusively in my pattern designs, but whatever you choose consider one that does not stretch or shrink as the best choice of foundation for this project.

shrink as the best choice of foundation for this project. Allow an extra 4" margin around the three-piece pattern for attaching to your frame. Transfer the enlargement onto your backing of choice with a Sanford brand Sharpie or Rub-A-Dub using your preferred method of transfer. I also recommend that the entire piece of rug backing fabric be serged or zigzagged.

To prevent the backing from raveling during the finishing steps, the following is recommended: Mark a line 2" above the top edges of the front and back pieces (this allowance folds over pillow cording for a whipped edge), then zigzag on each side of that line. On the sides and bottom of each piece, mark a line for the seam allowance $1/2$" outside the tote edge and zigzag on each side of that line. On the tote base, mark a $1/2$" seam allowance outside the base shape and zigzag on each side of that line. Mark the center of each piece as well as the handle placement marks on your backing as shown on the tote art.

The enlarged paper pattern will also be used for making the tote lining but the seam allowances need to be added for the lining, which will be covered later in the instructions.

Hooking the Tote

Hook the tote pieces taking care to stay **inside** the line defining the shape of the tote piece. (Hooking **on** or **over** the line will prevent the pieces from seaming together properly.) Using various dark background strips, outline one row around the entire tote piece (top edge, sides, bottom edge). Notice how some stems and vines on the tote front piece continue onto the tote back

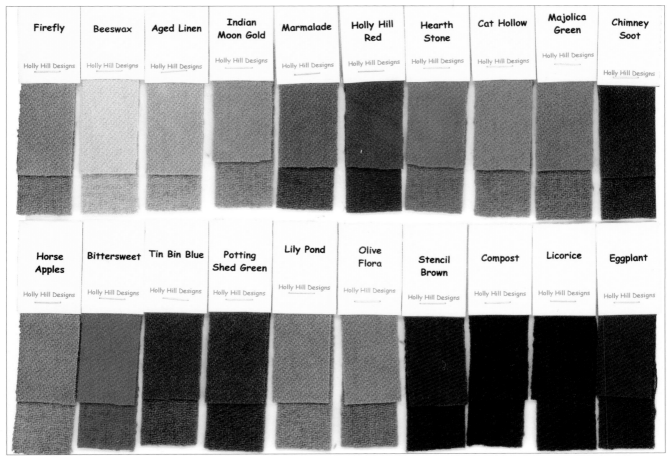

Wool samples used for hooking *Fantasy Garden Tote*.

piece. Pulling the loops extra high on some of the flower centers adds texture and interest. Create other interesting centers by mixing small bits of brighter colors like Bittersweet, Horse Apples, and Tin Bin Blue dyed over herringbones and small glen plaids. On some flowers I hooked a beaded center by holding two different color strips together, hooking alternately from each color. Consider combining strips of several textures and hues of green to create a leaf, made even more interesting by adding a contrasting vein. A tightly woven, as-is wool with a dominant narrow stripe, cut into strips adds visual interest in the bird's tail. In summary, visual interest can be created by including some lights, darks, brights, and some dulls.

The dark background, when viewed as a whole, appears to be off-black but actually is a mixture of many darks. I dyed dark dye formulas like Chimney Soot, Stencil Brown, Compost, Licorice, and Eggplant over assorted textures like gray and camel herringbones, small checks,

and glen plaids. I also added dark solids and textures of dark green and navy. Strips were cut from all these various colors and textures and then hooked in random directions.

Finishing

When the tote pieces have been hooked, check the backside to see if there are any empty spaces, as well as making any final color changes. Then proceed with the following steps for the finishing and construction.

1. Block face down, heavily. Let dry and repeat if necessary.

2. When dry, apply a thin coat of MCG Textiles brand rug backing with a narrow brush onto the wrong side covering the outside row of loops, but not onto the unhooked backing fabric that will be used in the seaming. The rug backing smells like latex paint, is the consistency of sour cream, and cleans up with water. Let dry completely.

FRONT

BASE

BACK

3. It is important to remember at this point to be sure that a 2" seam allowance has been added at the top edges and ¹/₂" along all sides and bottom before trimming away excess backing. Beginning at the 2" marked seam allowance at the top edges, trim away excess foundation fabric outside the zigzagged rows.

4. Finger-press all seam allowances toward backside as close as possible to the last row of hooking (one thread of backing will still show.) There will be some fullness around the edges of the tote bottom.

5. Pin tote front and back pieces wrong sides together with large safety pins, aligning edges.

6. Use yarn or wool strips to whip the two edges together. Securely tacking ends.

7. Attach the tote base in the same manner, matching center marks with side seams and using safety pins to hold the base and sides together while whipping the edges. Ease any extra fullness of the seam allowance around curves.

8. Along top edge, fold the 2" seam allowance over narrow ³/₁₆"-diameter pillow cording and whip with yarn or wool strips.

Handle Construction

Make two handles. For short handles as shown on my tote, cut two pieces of wool each measuring 3¹/₂" x 14¹/₂". If you prefer longer shoulder straps, lengthen accordingly.

1. With right sides together, stitch a ¹/₄" seam at each end (**Shown in Figure 1**) so that the opening between is 10¹/₂".

2. Using "jumbo" or ¹/₂"-diameter pillow cording, wrap a small piece of masking tape around ends so they do not unravel and then cut 2 lengths that are 10¹/₂" long. Note that in order to avoid bulkiness, the cording is not in the part of the handle that is attached to the inside of the tote.

3. Fold the two raw edges of the wool handle toward the centerline with the edges touching. Place the cording segment over the raw edges in the center opening of the handle (**Shown in Figure 2**).

4. Bring the folded edges together over the cording, pin in place, and hand-stitch together (with craft thread) starting and ending over the length of the cording only. Notice on **Figure 3** that the ends of the handle are flat.

5. Pin handles to handle placement marks, hold flat ends of handles on the inside of the tote so they extend $1^1/_2$" below the top edge. Use heavy button/craft thread to attach handle to the inside of tote top edge. Securely sew several tacking stitches between the rows of hooking, as well as close to the top whipped edge and they will not show on the front.

Lining

Use the paper pattern enlargement and add $^1/_2$" seam allowance all around. Pin pattern to wool and cut out lining pieces. Sew side seams and seam around base. (The lining needs to be slightly smaller than the tote to prevent gathers.) Trim and clip edges. Make a pocket if you want one.

Insert lining inside tote, turn under top edge of lining, and slipstitch next to whipped edge. Make hidden tacking stitches through lining and tote side seams to flatten and secure the lining in place. ●

Designer's Tip:

As purists, we rug hookers wouldn't dream of applying paint-on rug backing on our soon-to-be-heirloom rugs ... but, to keep hooked strips from snagging on a hard-wearing tote plus adding stability, it has an advantage worth considering.

Figure 1

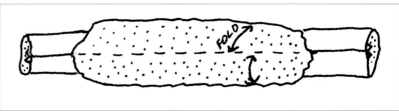

Figure 2

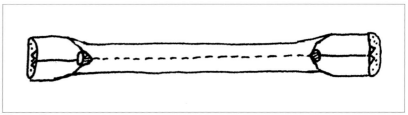

Figure 3

ARTIST: SUSAN QUICKSALL

Susan Quicksall has been designing and teaching various needle arts for more than 25 years. She is the owner of Holly Hill Designs, a rug hooking pattern and hand-painted needlepoint design business, and teaches rug hooking in adult continuing education classes at the local junior college and at workshops. She is founding member of Bluebonnet Rug Hookers in Waco, Texas, an ATHA Chapter certified in 2004. Susan has recently published her dye formulas in a booklet with color swatches, Mellow Colors for Rug Hooking Using Pro-Chem Dyes. *Susan's work has been featured in* Rug Hooking *and* A Celebration of Hand-Hooked Rugs, *in three consecutive publications.*

Her areas of special interest are #6 and #7-cut shaded primitives, color combinations, and pictorials. Susan lives with her husband, Doug, in their country home in central Texas.

A Slice of Summer

BY JENNY RUPP AND LISA YEAGO, THE POTTED PEAR

This blackbird on a watermelon slice is a tribute to summer. Who doesn't like a sweet, juicy slice of watermelon? This pattern is easy to enlarge or reduce, depending on where you want to display it. You don't have to add the bird and just use it as a pillow, or you can display the entire piece on a shelf or a buffet for the summer. This project combines rug hooking and needle felting, however appliqué can be substituted for making the seeds, and the bird can be made from sewing wool pieces together. Embellish the bird with beads or little feathers. Use your imagination to make this piece your own.

Watermelon, 23" x 7¹/₂", and **Blackbird,** 4" x 9", #8-cut wool on linen. Designed and hooked by Jenny Rupp and Lisa Yeago, The Potted Pear, Cincinatti, Ohio, 2005.

WHAT YOU NEED:

Red textured (herringbone, tweed) wool-center

- $3/8$-yard dark red
- $2/8$-yard medium red
- $1/8$-yard light red

Green textured wool-rind

- $2/8$-yard dark green
- $1/8$-yard medium green
- $1/8$-yard light green

Black textured wool-blackbird

- $1/8$-yard dark black
- $1/16$-yard medium black

Gold wool - blackbird eye and beak, 1' x 13' piece

- 1 yard linen for hooking

- Dark brown roving for big seeds or 2" x 22" piece of brown wool
- 8" dowel rod
- Antique brown craft paint
- Fiberfil or fabric scraps for stuffing
- Strong black thread or string

Equipment:

- Basic rug hooking supplies
- Sewing machine
- Large needle
- Scissors
- Glue gun
- Felting needle and foam block

Instructions:

1. Enlarge your pattern onto paper and trace with a black marker. Lay the linen backing over the paper pattern and trace. Remember to reverse the bird pattern so you will have two sides. Allow 3" or 4" of excess linen for each piece. Sew a straight stitch directly on the black line of the pattern for each piece. Measure out 1" and sew another line around each piece. These two lines will ensure the hooked piece will not fray or come apart when clipping in close to lash pieces together. Do this for the three watermelon pieces and for the two blackbird pieces. Hook each piece according to the pattern.

2. For the watermelon slice, hook in the following order:
   - **Side Piece:** 2 rows dark green, 1 row light green, dark red, medium red, and light red.
   - **Bottom Piece:** dark green for the majority of the piece, light green for inside or spot shapes, and then surround that with medium green. Add some strips of medium green throughout the dark green to give some interest.
   - Stay inside the lines when you hook each piece. Do not steam the finished pieces. Before lashing the pieces together, hold the pieces up to each other to make sure the rind lines match. This is the time to adjust your pieces if they do not fit together. You may have to pull out a line of hooking or add one so that the pieces are the same size. If you hook right inside the lines of the pattern, this should not be a problem.

3. To assemble the blackbird, first cut away the excess linen to the 1" line. Make the beak by cutting out a 1" square of gold wool and folding it over on the diagonal. Stitch along one open side; come around the corner and before sewing it shut, stuff a tiny bit of Fiberfil inside to plump out the beak. Set aside the beak. Thread the large needle with strong black string or thread. Starting at the base of the bird, begin to lash the pieces together.
   - **Lashing Method:** Hold the excess linen between your thumb and first finger. This should draw two hooked pieces tightly together in your hand. Take your needle and thread and lash the two pieces snugly together. Lash between loops, not through loops. Join the pieces through every loop or so. If the pieces are pulled snugly together, no backing should show.
   - When you get to the beak, insert it in between the body and stitch it together with the body pieces. Leave a small hole in the bottom for stuffing. Stuff the bird and sew shut, leaving just a small space for the dowel rod. Do not overstuff. Overstuffing will expand the loops

Beak pattern

- Fold over on the diagonal. See body of instructions for completion and assembly.

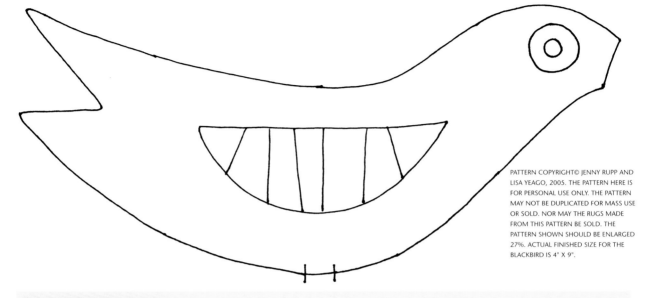

Blackbird Pattern

- Make two—reverse one to create both sides of the bird.
- Striped wing—hook alternating light and dark black wool, ending with lighter black on both ends of wings.
- Hook one strip of gold around the eye and hook one loop for the center of the eye.
- Leave a small hole at the base of the blackbird for inserting the dowel rod.

Designer's Tip:

Attaching hooked pieces together can be made easier by using textured wool. Individual loops are not as noticeable when textured wool is used as when solid wool is used and lashing stitches seem to hide among textured loops. If you want to combine the wool, try to keep the solid wool away from the areas that will be stitched together.

too much and backing will show. Set bird aside.

4. To assemble the watermelon cut away the excess linen to the 1" line. Sew the top of the watermelon pieces together. Remember to leave a small hole open for the dowel to be inserted. Use the same lashing method as for the bird. Take the base rind piece and lash it to one side completely. Now lash the base rind piece to the other side, but start at one side, stop half way and knot. Go back to the other edge and work your way to the bottom. Leave a large enough hole to stuff and then lash completely shut. Do not overstuff the watermelon.

- **Hint**: It is nice to use fabric scraps to stuff the watermelon. It gives it a heavier stuffing that makes the watermelon more stable and sub-

stantial and allows the blackbird to balance nicely on top.

5. Needle felting the large seeds is simple. Take some brown roving and pull off a 2" or so piece. Position it over the thick foam block. With quick, up and down plunges, poke the roving with the needle until a firm shape takes place. Pull the seed up from the block and keep shaping it with the needle. Once you have a nice, firm seed shape, attach it to the hooked watermelon with the same, quick stabbing motions. The model has 5 oversized seeds per side. See pattern for placement.

- **Hint**: If you do not have access to needle felting supplies, you can simply appliqué some wool seeds using the template provided on the pattern. The look will be similar. Just stitch them directly onto the hook-

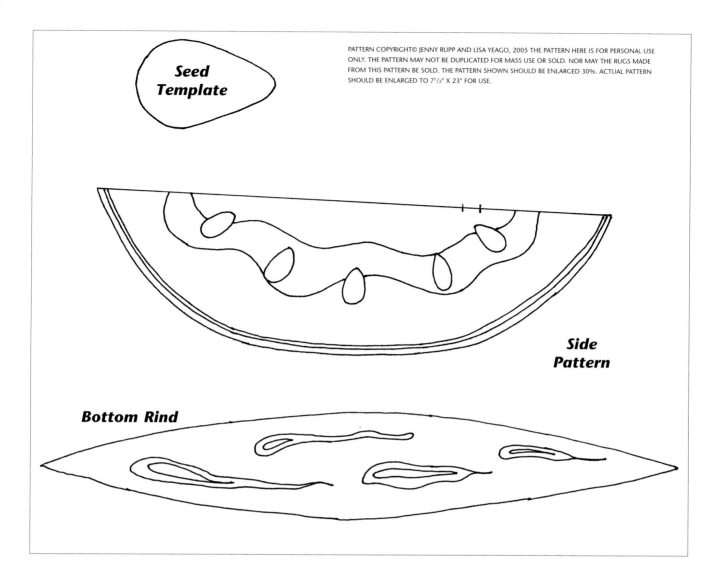

Seed Template

Side Pattern

Bottom Rind

ing with small stitches in matching brown thread.

6. To attach the blackbird to the watermelon take your antique brown craft paint and finger rub some onto the dowel rod. Allow to dry. Heat up the hot glue gun and then shove the painted dowel rod into the small hole at the base of the blackbird. Apply a small amount of hot glue to secure the blackbird onto the dowel rod. Shove the other end of the dowel into the hole at the top of the watermelon. The blackbird on the model sits 1^{1}/$_{4}$" above the watermelon slice. Apply some hot glue around the dowel in the watermelon to secure. ●

Watermelon Pattern

- Make two of the side pattern and enlarge to 11.5" long x 7.24" deep
- Make one bottom rind piece and enlarge to 29" long x 5.5" wide
- Seed template, actual size for making 10 seeds
- Leave small hole at the top for inserting the dowel rod
- Leave a small hole at the base of the blackbird for inserting the dowel rod.

ARTISTS: JENNY RUPP AND LISA YEAGO

Jenny Rupp and Lisa Yeago are frequent contributors to Rug Hooking *magazine. They own a rug design and supply business, The Potted Pear— based in West Chester, Ohio. They offer original rug designs, hand dyed wool and yarn, books on rug hooking techniques and patterns for dolls. They can be reached at: thepottedpear@fuse.net or at (513) 759–5301.*

Funky Hooked Belts

BY KATIE FISHBUNE

Belts are a "must have" item in most wardrobes and are currently quite trendy in the world of fashion. A unique one-of-a kind belt can set you apart from the crowd and be a fun way to use already cut strips of wool in a variety of cuts, colors, and textures. Have fun and create a lasting piece of tradional fiber art to wear for years to come. Some things to remember when using traditional rug hooking to make a belt include the following:

- Choose your buckle first. It determines the correct width for the finished belt
- Buckles can be removed from old belts. Check your own closet or local thrift stores or try the following online sources: *www.eleathersupply.com* or *www.ejoyce.com*. I found these (and many other) sites by doing a *www.google.com* search for "belt buckles." I ordered buckles ($0.99 to $2.50 each) from both sites and received them in less than a week.
- Belts can be made in any width and/or length. The three belts shown here are 41" length (excluding buckle), which fits over my favorite jeans that have a somewhat low rise and allows for a comfortable—several inch overlap. Make your belt the length of a well fitting belt you already own or use a tape measure to decide how long it should be.
- Hook low. Added bulk at your waist and/or hips is NOT desirable! Also, the belt will fit through the belt loops easier if it is less bulky.
- A hooked belt does not require a lot of wool. It is an excellent way to use up already cut strips from other projects. In addition, using solids, textures, and mixed cuts is a great way to add more interest to a hooked belt. Mixed cuts make this project particularly eye-catching—cut your #6 or #8 cuts in half with a scissors for #3 or #4 cuts. A small project is a great place to experiment with those smaller cuts, which can give much more detail to your work. Backgrounds can be hooked easily with #6-8 cuts.
- In addition, all these belts were made with a #4 cut used as the outside outline of the pattern allowing more space for the individual designs elements or motifs to show.
- Linen or monk's cloth are recommended rather than burlap since they are more pliable and hold up much better over time. There is nothing worse than to spend time, energy, and money creating something special that doesn't last long enough due to "FFF" (foundation fabric failure)!

The following supplies/instructions explain how to make the cream colored *Floral Vine* belt, the black *Funky Shape* belt, and the blue *Hit or Miss* denim belt. Use these as a starting point to create your own wonderful designs.

Left to Right: Hit or Miss, Funky Shape, and **Floral Vine belts.** 41" x 1¹/₂"–2", #3–8 cuts of wool on linen. Designed and hooked by Katie Fishbune, St. Charles, Illinois, 2005.

Supplies:

- **Buckle** - 2" wide for the *Floral Vine* belt or the *Funky Shape* belt; 1¹/₂" for the *Hit or Miss* belt.
- **Linen backing** in a size wide enough to fit on your frame or in your hoop and long enough to fit the length of your belt. I hook several belts on the same piece of linen keeping them about 2" apart to allow for finishing. This keeps waste to a minimum.
- **Wool strips** in assorted sizes (#3 through #8), colors, and textures. Use leftover strips from other projects if possible. For the *Floral Vine* belt a variety of light colored wools are needed equal to about 1/4 yard for the background and small scraps and pieces in greens, blues, and reds for the leaves, vines, and flowers. The *Funky Shape* belt requires a variety of dark wools equal to about ¹/₄ yard for the background and assorted blues, reds, golds, greens, and purples for the funky shapes. The *Hit or Miss* denim belt requires various blues (and a bit of teal for a little "spark" or "poison") equal to about a total of ¹/₄ yard of fabric.

- ¹/₈ **yard of 45" cotton fabric** to coordinate with the belt's color plan. For the *Floral Vine* belt a cream colored fabric with green leaves, vines, and red flowers was used. For the *Funky Shapes* belt a black fabric with dots of yellow, orange, red, and green was used. For the *Hit or Miss* belt a diamond fabric in two values of blue with scrolls of black was used.
- **Thread** to match belt/lining color
- **Awl** to make belt holes
- **Perle cotton** (size 5) in a color, which coordinates with the hooked belt
- **Hand sewing needles** with an eye large enough to accept the perle cotton

Instructions:

1. Determine the length and width of the desired belt.
2. Adjust the width of the belt according to your measurements and transfer the design to linen for *Floral Vine* or *Funky Shape* belts. Adjust the length of the design by eliminating or adding design elements to reach the desired size. For example, on the *Floral Vine* belt, lengthen the vine at points where the

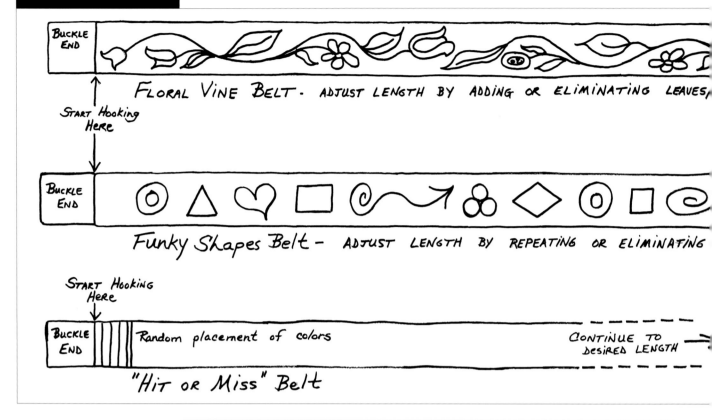

A hooked belt does not require a lot of wool— it is an excellent way to use up already cut strips from other projects.

vine is broken and add additional leaves or flowers. Draw the design on the linen for the *Hit or Miss* design to the desired size. It is imperative that the edges of all the belts be on the straight grain of the linen.

3. Starting at one end of the belt pattern, complete all hooking in a 4–5" long area by following the following guidelines for individual belt designs:

Guidelines for Individual Designs

Floral Vine belt: Hook outside the outline of the belt in light cream colored wools (#4 cut); using a variety of cut sizes. Hook vine in brownish green color; hook leaves in greens with vines in assorted colors; hook flowers alternating reds and blues. Fill in remainder of the background with light colored wools.

Funky Shape belt: Hook the outline of the belt in dark colored wools (# 4 cut) using a variety of cut sizes. Hook shapes in a random mix of left-over wool strips. Try to use each color about three times throughout the belt in a pleasing arrangement. Fill in remainder of background with dark wools.

Hit or Miss belt: Hook outside outline of belt in a middle value blue color—not too light or too dark (cut in a size #4); hook a variety of cut sizes and blue values as randomly pulled from a bag.

1. Complete hooking on the entire design area of the belt.

2. On the end where the buckle will be, leave a $1^{1}/_{2}$" tail, which will be hand sewn to secure the buckle (see #8 below). Serge or zigzag stitch approximately $^{1}/_{2}$" to $^{5}/_{8}$" from hooked edge of design.

3. Steam belt and allow to dry thoroughly.

ALS AT VINE BREAKS

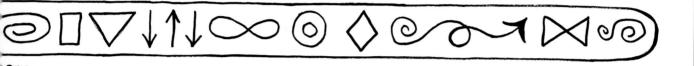

PES

BELT PATTERNS

Tips for Designing & Color Planning More Belts

- Coordinate your belt with a favorite shirt, blouse, or dress. Use elements such as flowers, paisleys, or geometric designs found in the piece. Use similar colors found in the article of clothing.

- Choose the fabric lining for the belt first and then design the belt with elements and colors from the fabric.

- Hook a special belt for that "little black dress" using metallic cording, beads and antique buttons. This would be a great opportunity to use other fabrics such as silks or shiny specialty yarns left over from knitting projects.

- Hook a belt for your teenager (or for yourself to wear to their athletic events) with their high school name or initials, logo, and colors. (For our school— St. Charles East Fighting Saints—a black belt with the initials STCE surrounded by orange fleur-de-lis would be appropriate.)

- Hook a belt for a child with their favorite sports team name or favorite cartoon character.

- *Hit or Miss* belts can be done in any monochromatic color scheme or using every color in a rainbow. You could also change the direction of the hooking in a "hit or miss" belt so it runs end-to-end or so you have blocks of vertical hooking alternating with blocks of horizontal hooking.

- Hook a belt to coordinate with a hooked purse or hat.

- Hook a collar for your dog ³/₄" or 1" wide with paw prints or bones utilizing these techniques.

- Let your imagination run wild—you are more creative than you can even dream!

Hook a special belt for that "little black dress" using metallic cording, beads and antique buttons. This would be a great opportunity to use other fabrics such as silks or shiny specialty yarns left over from knitting projects.

4. Turn unfinished edge of linen to the back of the belt as close to hooking as possible; steam belt again and allow to dry.

5. Measure finished belt size length/width and tear cotton fabric for belt lining to that size *plus* $^1/2$" on all sides. For example, if your hooked belt measures 2" by 41", tear fabric 3" by 42". Turn over $^1/2$" on one long side and one short side of lining fabric and iron. Add buckle to belt by pushing prong through the belt between rows of hooking and fold over linen to the back of the belt. Make sure a row of hooking is on each side of the prong. Pin in place. Hand stitch this linen "tail" securely. Lay the lining on the hooked belt with wrong sides facing together. Adjust so the turned over corner matches the belt exactly at the buckle end and hand sew the lining to the belt as close as possible to the last row of hooked loops. Do not allow any of the backing linen to show. After sewing these two sides, turn under the remaining two sides of the lining and hand stitch as close as possible to the last row of hooked loops. Again, **do not allow any of the linen backing to show and do not allow any of the lining fabric to show from the front of the belt.**

6. Put on the belt and determine where the main hole for the prong should be and mark with a pin. With an awl, gently push between rows of hooking and through the lining fabric—try to push the threads apart rather than breaking them. Continue to push the awl through until a generous hole has been stretched. Using perle cotton (doubled through the needle) in a color that blends with the hooking in the area of the hole and satin stitch about $^3/8$" around the hole pulling tightly. Reinsert the awl as necessary to keep the hole open as the stitching is completed. Repeat this process to make two additional belt holes 2" away from either side of the main hole.

7. Steam the finished belt one more time, especially the end without the buckle. This area should be flattened as much as possible to fit through the buckle easily. ●

ARTIST: KATIE FISHBUNE

Katie Fishbune's love of art, color, and fiber began in early childhood, but her exposure to a traditional rug hooking workshop in 1990, resulted in a small hooked coaster and a subscription to Rug Hooking *magazine. After a move to St. Charles, Illinois in 1996, Katie found a wonderful teacher and mentor, Sue Hamer, who happened to live on the other side of St. Charles. After attending Sue's classes for several years, Katie became a certified McGown teacher. She is a member of the National Guild of Pearl K. McGown Rug Hookcrafters and a founding member of the ATHA Foxy Lady Rug Hookers Guild. Katie currently teaches rug hooking classes in her home studio in St. Charles and has taught classes and workshops in various parts of the country.*

Rose and Bud Eyeglass Case

PRIMITIVE SPIRIT DESIGN BY KAREN KAHLE

America's history of needle arts is filled with precious artifacts crafted by women to fill their workaday world with beauty. Stitched with love and ingenuity, needle cases, bags, pockets, and pincushions festooned with bits of fabric and threads were beloved companions at the worktable.

As much as I love art for art's sake, I also love creating practical projects that serve a function just as my foremothers did. I created this design after searching for just the right eyeglass case and not finding anything special. Since I am always looking for ways to include something that I have hooked in my daily routine, having this little case lets me see my hooking everyday. I am always drawn to floral motifs, and my favorite is the rose. This rose and bud design reminds me of the late summer garden, when every bloom seems like a precious gift. Since it is a small project, make up several in different colors. It also makes a nice travel bag for sewing scissors or other tools.

Rose and Bud Eyeglass Case, 6³/₄" x 3¹/₂", #8-cut wool on linen. Designed and hooked by Karen Kahle, Eugene, Oregon, 2005.

Designer Tips On Color

- Choose colors that compliment each other and that are different in value to make the motifs stand out. For the eyeglass case I have used the complementary colors red and green as the color scheme. Light values of red are played against dark values of green.

- The background is hooked with deep and dark values of green and includes many colors that are similar to green which add sparkle: olive, dark khaki, brown, hunter green, black and deep blues. I threw in a few plaids with unexpected colors and hooked them along the edge of the design for surprise. As long as the values of all these colors are dark, they will blend together. Mix them up as you hook them and keep lines of each color short. Short rows blend better than long lines of color.

- The flower motifs are hooked with light values of red, which should be all different kinds of colors in the pink family—peachy and rosy, as well as faded-out pink and light camel colors. Take time to find an exciting texture or two for the center of the rose, blending all varieties of red in deeper shades. This draws your eye to it and makes it the focal point.

- Keep the stems and foliage light to medium in value, making these elements of the design secondary in importance to the flower and bud. Use dusty tans, light khaki, celery, sage, and deeper camel colors. You can get more color variety if you use only a few loops of each color.

- A small project such as this is the perfect opportunity to try something different. See how many different colors of similar value you can make blend in your background. It helps to stand back from your design from time to time. This way you can better see what is blending in or standing out.

Hooking Fabrics

This is such a small project that you will be able to use leftover scraps of wool, perhaps from your strip bag. A total of a 1/4-yard of pieces of deep green and other similar colors are needed for the background. The flowers use scraps of light to medium pinks and reds as well as several medium values of neutrals. The leaves are hooked with very neutral colored light to medium greens, like sage, bronze, and deep camel.

Hooking Tips

I have hooked this design in a #8-cut of wool, but it would be lovely in a #6 or #7, or perhaps in a mixture of all three cuts. When combining cuts keep the height of all the loops the same height as the widest cut. Keep in mind that since this is to be an eyeglass case, it is preferable to keep the height of the loops a little on the shorter side, making the finished piece less bulky.

Stay within the motif lines as you hook, working the background along with the foreground. As much as you may want to get a lot of detail in such a small project, resist the temptation to hook more loops than needed. The bulk of over packing loops not only makes the finished piece heavy and bulky, but it distorts the proportions of the design. Consider using narrower cuts for some detail, or simply hooking one

Designer Tips On Finishing with Glue

- Finishing can be the crowning glory to a project, so taking your time to get the technique right can make all the difference in the world. Gluing makes an easy and fast finish to this hooking project. Fabric glue is convenient because you can glue right up to the edges of your hooking; otherwise it is difficult to hand sew multiple seams together and get close to both hooked edges. I do not recommend using a hot glue gun as it is difficult to control the flow of the hot glue, which may leave it highly visible on the finished piece.

- The trick is to not use too much fabric glue or else it will spurt out of the seams and show when it is dry. Keep a damp paper towel nearby to clean your fingers and the glue bottle tip. Apply only a thin line of glue so that when you press the two surfaces together glue doesn't bleed out.

- Fabri-tac sets up quickly which makes it an excellent choice. It also is high in tack, which makes it tricky to control (kind of like stringy mozzarella!). Another bonus is that it is permanent even when washed. With this in mind it is safer to wear an apron to protect your clothes.

- Tacky glue is easier to control, however it sets up slower and doesn't adhere quite as readily as Fabri-tac does. Experiment on a scrap of wool with both and see which one you are most comfortable with. You may find that attaching the finishing strip of pearl cotton at the end is easier when you apply an occasional dab of Tacky glue with a toothpick along the seam line.

or two less loops than you would normally. Hooking without packing loops will make the project lie flatter. It also retains the integrity of every loop, showing off the beauty of each fabric.

Finishing Instructions

1. After hooking both sides of the design, steam press it on the wrong side and fold the piece in half, following the pattern line; lightly steam press to make a crease. Hand sew a strip of wool in the middle of the crease line with a running stitch to cover the fold, leaving ¹/₂" tail hanging off on either end.

Trim the backing fabric to ¹/₂" and iron it under so that no backing is showing on the front; glue the seam in place. Glue the wool strip tails to the inside on top of the glued seams; let completely dry.

WHAT YOU NEED:

Finishing Materials:

- Needle and thread
- Scissors
- Pins
- Fabri-tac® or Tacky® fabric glue

- One 9" square of felted black flannel weight wool
- #5 black pearl cotton scrap or other small black cording

2. Create the wool lining. Open the hooked piece and center it on the black felted wool square. Trim the wool ¹/₂" away from all hooked edges. Fold the black wool in half inside of the folded hooked piece creating a sandwich. Smooth out any wrinkles in the wool.

With your scissors snip the black wool at the creased edge close to the edge of your hooking.

Finishing steps for assembling the *Rose and Bud Eyeglass Case.*

3. Using pins to hold the wool in place as you go, run a thin line of fabric glue along all the hooked edges, wrapping the black wool over the top of this edge so that no backing fabric is showing. When the glue is set remove the pins. Trim the wool close to the top of the loops of hooking.

4. Glue the sides and bottom of eyeglass case together using a thin line of glue placed about ¹/₂" away from the side edges and the top open edge; hold together with pins as needed. When the glue is dry, cover the glued seam with one strand of #5 black pearl cotton, lightly gluing in several places to hold it securely. ●

ARTIST: KAREN KAHLE

Karen Kahle considers herself a wool painter. Her painting and a love for impressionistic art and antique textiles have influenced her style. It is with a spirit of adventure that she brings new ideas and inspiration to her craft. Karen started her business, Primitive Spirit, six years ago with a dozen designs, which has grown to be a catalog of over 60 rugs. She has authored six books and written many articles on primitive style and color for Rug Hooking *magazine and other publications. Her latest projects include her own line of punch needle embroidery patterns, and a video called Color Inspiration For Primitive Hooked Rugs. For further information on Karen's rugs contact Primitive*

Spirit, PO Box 1363, Eugene, OR 97440, (541) 344-4316, www.primitivespiritrugs.com.

Old Saint Nick

BY KRIS MILLER

Old Saint Nick is a charming wall hanging inspired by the designs of old Christmas postcards from the turn of the century. It was hooked entirely with textured wool in #6 and #8 cut strips and wool roving for the beard which adds a touch of whimsy to your holiday décor.

Old Saint Nick, 18" x 23", #6 and 8-cut wool on linen. Designed and hooked by Kris Miller, Howell, Michigan, 2005.

WHAT YOU NEED:

- 26" x 31" piece of linen or monk's cloth

- Primitive rug hook

- Rug hooking frame (not a hoop)

- 6" x 15" peach or flesh colored textured wool for face, cut in #6

- 4–16" strips of brick herringbone texture for outline of nose, eyelids and mouth, cut in #6

- 1–16" strip of dark blue plaid for eyes, cut in #6

- 38" x 16" taupe and brown plaid over-dyed with Long John Red, a Vermont Folk Rugs color, for St. Nick's robe. Cut in #8

- 20" x 16^1/$_2$" maroon/olive plaid for outline of robe and mitten (segregate the olive shades in the plaid to hook the mitten). Cut in #8

- 14" x 16" taupe and cream check for fur collar, cut in #8

- 8" X 17" dark evergreen for outline of tree, cut in #6

- 26" x 16" houndstooth plaid over-dyed in an evergreen shade for filling the tree, cut in #8

- 1 – 16" strip of soft yellow for doll's hair, cut in #6

- 2 or 3 – 16" strips of light colored wool for doll's face and hand, cut in #6

- Scraps of gold strips for spots on doll's hat and buttons on shirt, cut in either #6 or #8

- Scraps of black for doll's eyes and scrap of red for doll's mouth, cut in #6

- 2–16" strips light blue or turquoise texture for doll's collar, cut in #6

- 3" x 15" medium blue texture for doll's shirt and hat, cut in #6

- 3" x 17" dark blue plaid for doll's pants, cut in #8

- ^{1}/$_2$ yard of light creamy colored texture for inside background, cut in #8

- ^{1}/$_2$ yard of gold herringbone for outside border background, cut in #8

- 3 shades of red for holly berries, cut in #8:
  - ❋ 5 strips of bright red/orange
  - ❋ 3 strips of flag red
  - ❋ 3 strips of the same red used in St. Nick's robe

- 4 shades of green for holly leaves, cut in #6:
  - ❋ 6" x 17" of the same evergreen shade used to outline the tree
  - ❋ 8" x 16" brighter shade of olive green
  - ❋ 4" x 15" grayed olive green
  - ❋ 6"x 18"dark green tweed

- 35 to 40 yards of worsted weight yarn for whipping the rug's edges

- 2^1/$_2$ yards of twill tape for hemming rug

- 3^1/$_2$ to 4 ounces of creamy white Lincoln roving for St. Nick's beard. Roving is available for purchase through Spruce Ridge Studios

All wool measurements are approximate. Your results may vary depending on how high or low you hook.

Hooking the Wool Strips

1. Trace the pattern onto a 26" x 31" piece of backing with a permanent marker. These measurements allow for an extra 4" margin around all sides of the pattern. I hooked my wall hanging on primitive linen.

2. Start with the face by hooking the eyelids in the brick texture. Hook the blue plaid eyes in a semicircle by following the contour of the eyelids. (Don't worry about putting the highlights in his eyes right now; you will do that a little later). Continue by hooking the eyebrows and nose in the brick texture. Now fill in the face with the flesh colored wool.

3. Hook St. Nick's hood. Outline with the maroon/olive plaid and fill with red. When cutting the maroon/olive plaid, set aside about 8 to 10 strips which contain the most olive green

color and 2 or 3 strips which contain the most gold color. These will be used for hooking his mitten.

4. With the taupe and cream check, outline and hook the fur collar. Use a small leftover strip and hook the highlight in each eye. To give St. Nick a "twinkle," just pull up two ends (no loop) through the blue plaid and trim even with your work.

5. Outline the tree in evergreen and fill it in with the evergreen plaid.

6. Outline St. Nick's arm and body with maroon/olive plaid. Outline his mitten with the segregated gold strips and fill with the olive green set aside previously. Hook the red in St. Nick's arm.

7. Hook the doll. Refer to the supply list for the colors that are used. Begin by hooking the doll's hair and face. Next hook the hat. Hook the collar and then the doll's shirt. Use the same

wool as the doll's face to hook the hand. Hook the pants last. Now go back with a black scrap and hook the doll's eyes by pulling up two ends of the strip (just as you did for St. Nick's eyes) and trimming them even. Hook the doll's mouth in red with the same technique. Continue doing the same by hooking several gold spots on the doll's hat and the two buttons on the front of the doll's shirt.

8. Finish hooking the red in St. Nick's body, hooking around the doll, the tree branches, and the fur collar.

9. Hook the holly leaves. I hooked them in a #6 to get crisp points on the leaves. I chose either the grayed olive or bright olive for one side of the leaf and hooked the evergreen or dark green tweed for the remaining side of the leaf. Make sure to always use a contrasting green when hooking leaves that overlap, i.e. use a brighter olive

Separating wool roving

green for the side of a leaf that overlaps the dark side of another leaf.

10. Hook the holly berries in the 3 varieties of red. Just pull up a few loops in a random fashion to form an oval shape. They don't have to be perfectly round! Hook some of the background wool around the berries to hold their shape.

11. Hook and fill in the inside background around St. Nick with the light creamy texture. I used a color that

Designer's Tips

• Hooking with roving is done in much the same way as if you were to hook with a wide cut fabric strip.

• Always use a primitive hook, so you are less likely to split the fibers when pulling up the loops.

• Always bring the ends to the top of your work and trim even.

• When you end the roving strip, begin a new piece in the same opening, just as you would do for a fabric strip.

• Each time a loop of roving is pulled up, roll your hook toward the previous loop. This will help keep the previous loop from being pulled out.

• Space the loops at least 2 to 3 threads apart. Don't worry if the loops are not perfectly even. Don't pack your loops.

• Outline the design and then fill it in.

• Roving can have different textures depending on what type of sheep it came from. Lincoln roving can be "slippery" compared to other types of roving. Take your time with your hooking and the results will be great!

reminded me of paper that has dulled over the years.

12. Hook and fill the outside border with the gold herringbone. Many old postcards had gold accents and this reminded me of a tarnished gold trim.

13. After hooking all the fabric strips, steam the piece with a steam iron and a damp press cloth, front and back, set it aside, and let it dry flat for 24 hours. The hooked roving will not need to be steamed and it is better to do this step now before proceeding.

You have probably noticed that St. Nick's beard has not been hooked yet. It is better to leave this hooking to do at the very end for several reasons. First, as the roving is hooked, it will fluff out and fill in the hooking area. It is much easier to hook the roving up against wool strips for this reason. Secondly, I prefer to minimize the exposure of the wool roving against the carding strips of my rug hooking frame as much as possible. The carding strips can tear and pull at the roving so extra caution is needed when stretching a roving-hooked area over the prickle strips. If you are using a rug hooking frame with an open hooking area of about 10"x 13¹/₂", you should be able to center the area of the beard on your frame, and it can be hooked entirely without moving your work.

Hooking with Roving

Roving is the clean and combed wool from a fiber-bearing animal. It is usually a long fluffy "rope" that is several inches in diameter. I chose wool roving that came from the fleece of a Lincoln sheep. It had a creamy light vanilla color and a hairy texture that reminded me of Santa's beard. To prepare the roving for hooking, you must do several preliminary steps:

• Roving comes in a long, loose "rope." Grasp it in your hands and pull off a piece of about 18" in length. The ends will look wispy. Hold the piece by the wispy end in your two hands and gently pull it apart lengthwise. It will separate into two smaller pieces. (**See picture**)

• Grasp this smaller half piece of roving in both hands, with your hands about 6" apart. **Gently pull** so that you can feel the fibers just begin to pull apart, **but do not separate the fiber**. Reposition your hands farther down the roving and repeat. This will gently open up the fibers so the roving will be a little fluffier and easier to hook (if you are a spinner, you will recognize this procedure as "pre-drafting"). If the roving is accidentally apart, just set aside the smaller piece to use later. This smaller, fluffier piece will be about the diameter of a Sharpie marker. Strips of roving about the diameter of a pencil can also be used. The size of your hooked loops will depend upon the diameter of the roving strip. I wanted St. Nick's beard to have fatter, puffier loops.

• Now you are ready to hook with roving!

Hook St. Nick's mouth with a brick herringbone/texture fabric strip. Now hook a row of roving around St. Nick's hood, around the edge of the fur collar, and back up to where you started. Next hook a row of roving around St. Nick's face. My roving is hooked directionally under the nose to give an impression of a mustache. Now fill in the top part of the hair and then the beard last. You may wish to hook the beard directionally in a "U" pattern to give the feeling of the way the hair grows. For best results, try to hook the roving a little higher than the wool strips.

Once the roving has been completely hooked, the piece is ready to hem. Take it to your sewing machine and sew small straight stitches $^1/4$" from the finished edge, taking care not to catch the toe of the presser foot in the outermost row of loops. Use a zigzag stitch and sew on top of the row of straight stitching that was just sewn. Repeat this process $^1/4$" from the first row of stitching.

Use a worsted weight yarn that matches the outside border color. Thread the yarn through a bent tip tapestry needle. Work from the back of your hooking. I fold my linen over a scant $^1/4$", hold the twill tape next to the edge, and whip the wool yarn around the folded edge of the linen. I catch a small portion of the twill tape while I am whipping, thus finishing the edge and attaching the twill tape at the same time. After I have finished whipping with the yarn, I trim away any excess linen to within 1" of my hooking and hand sew the other edge of the twill tape to the wall hanging with a slipstitch.

Old Saint Nick is now ready to be displayed along with your other holiday decorations. Hang him in a prominent spot so your guests can be impressed with your wonderful hooking abilities! ●

ARTIST: KRIS MILLER

Kris Miller is a self-taught rug hooker who started hooking seven years ago. She began to draw up her own patterns in those first years and soon began to sell them as a means to feed her pet goats. Her business, Spruce Ridge Studios, has blossomed into a successful pattern business that now represents many other artists. Kris also sells hand-dyed and as-is wool, rug hooks and accessories, and wool roving. Items may be purchased by mail order or by appointment to visit her studio. She exclusively teaches primitives and wide cuts with a heavy emphasis on textured wool with no shading. Additionally, Kris teaches mini-workshops every year on how to hook with roving. Kris's honors, awards, and accolades include Best of Show ribbons from her County Fair and; blue and second place ribbons at the Michigan State Fair; white and blue ribbons at Sauder Village, Archbold Ohio; an honorable mention in A Celebration of Hand-Hooked Rugs XIII *(2003); and an honorable mention in* Celebration of Hand-hooked Rugs XVI *(2006). She lives in Howell, Michigan with her husband, two sons, and an assortment of angora goats and sheep. Kris Miller, Spruce Ridge Studios, 1786 Eager Rd. , Howell, MI 48855, 517-546-7732, www.spruceridgestudios.com*

Hospitalitea Tea Cozy

BY DONNA HRKMAN

Combining the welcoming symbol of a pineapple with the social custom of relaxing with a "spot of tea" and sweets, my "Hospitalitea Tea Cozy" is a good way to bring people together. Dating back to the 1600s, tea cozies have been used as an accepted method of keeping teapots warm. At one time credit has been given to the English, Irish, Norwegians, and Danish for inventing the cozy. Wherever it began, the cozy has played an important role in the history of tea.

Hospitalitea Tea Cozy, 16"W x 14"H, #4 and #8-cut wool on linen. Designed and hooked by Donna Hrkman, Dayton, Ohio, 2005.

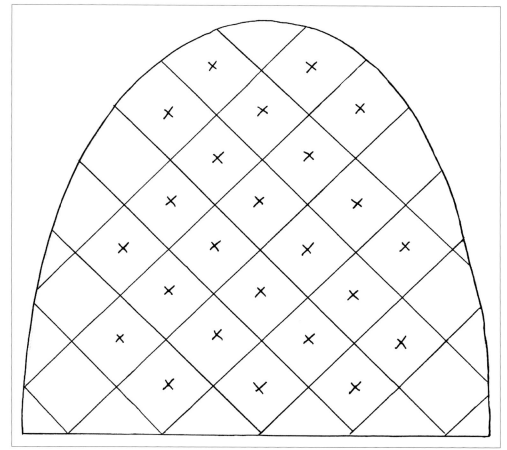

PATTERN COPYRIGHT© DONNA HRKMAN, 2005. THE PATTERN HERE IS FOR PERSONAL USE ONLY. THE PATTERN MAY NOT BE DUPLICATED FOR MASS USE OR SOLD. NOR MAY THE RUGS MADE FROM THIS PATTERN BE SOLD. ACTUAL PATTERN SIZE SHOULD BE ENLARGED TO 16"W X 14"H FOR USE.

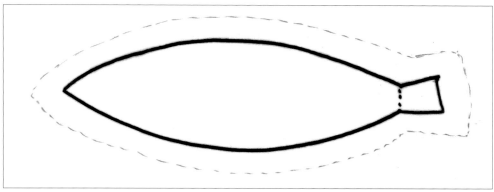

PATTERN COPYRIGHT© DONNA HRKMAN, 2005. THE PATTERN HERE IS FOR PERSONAL USE ONLY. THE PATTERN MAY NOT BE DUPLICATED FOR MASS USE OR SOLD. NOR MAY THE RUGS MADE FROM THIS PATTERN BE SOLD. PINEAPPLE LEAF PATTERN SHOULD BE ENLARGED 38%. EACH LEAF ACTUAL SIZE IS 5"L.

Directions

1. Cut linen and zigzag edges to prevent fraying. Lay unwashed linen piece on smooth, flat surface, center and transfer pineapple design onto it. Next, transfer the pattern, *Hospitalitea* onto the washed linen piece.

2. Trace leaf pattern onto piece of green wool, folded in half to make fronts and backs, enough for three finished leaves, two pieces per leaf. Leave $^{3}/_{8}$" border around each leaf.

3. Hook the pineapple pattern as shown, using the darker sets of colors at the bottom and working up to lighter colors at the top.

4. Cut $^{1}/_{8}$" or #4 size strips of the dark brown wool and pull short lengths (approximately $1^{1}/_{2}$") up through the centers of the hooked squares.

5. Hook the word "Hospitalitea" into the washed linen piece. Pull tails of wool strips up under the previous loop to keep lettering smooth.

You're going out for tea today, be careful what you do; let all accounts that I hear, be pleasant ones of you.—Kate Greenaway

6. Take finished pineapple piece and draw a line 1"around the design. Do the same for the *Hospitalitea* piece.

7. Sew around just ¹/₈" inside that drawn line to prevent fraying.

8. Trim extra fabric off both linen pieces. Pin cotton batting to the backside of *Hospitalitea* linen, keeping as smooth and even as possible. Baste ¹/₄" around the drawn line. Flip over; trim extra batting to within ¹/₄" of the basting line.

9. Take the fabric for the lining. Fold in half, right sides together, and use the cutout pineapple piece as a pattern to draw around onto the lining fabric. Use a straight selvedge edge if possible at the bottom of the pattern.

10. Sew curved arch edges of lining fabric together, leaving the straight bottom part open. Cut notches in the border

hospitalitea

outside the sewn line to allow lining to lie flat without bunching.

11. Sew leaf patterns along line, keeping a ³/₈" border around each leaf. Leave 1¹/₂"unsewn along the side of each leaf to allow turning and placement of the wire for stiffening. Clip seams, turn inside out, insert wire, and whip stitch the hole on the side closed. Lay leaves at top of pineapple and pin into place.

12. Pin front and back hooked pieces face-to-face. Do a test run on a scrap piece of linen to make sure machine tension and stitch length is correct. Carefully sew the front and back of the linen cozy together, making sure to keep hooked loops free of the needle. Using a blunt stiletto to scoot the loops tucked away from the needle is a good way to ensure a smooth line of stitching.

13. When the cozy is stitched together, turn right sides out. Take the stitched

...A friend you help to mend a heart, boost you toward a brand new start, school girl glee, share a quiet cup of tea.—Jan Miller Girando

lining, right side out, and slide it up into the cozy, matching up the seams. The bottom edges of the cozy and the lining should line up. Pin the lining to the linen cozy, leaving a 6" open area along the hooked front edge. Sew the lining to the hooked cozy.

14. Pull the lining out through the 6" gap. Tuck the lining up inside of the cozy, fitting it along the seam lines. Slipstitch the 6" gap closed, press lining along bottom edge of cozy. ●

ARTIST: DONNA HRKMAN

Donna Hrkman has been an artist most of her life, but she just learned rug hooking within the last four years. She earned a bachelor of fine arts degree in drawing and painting and has done her share of watercolors and oil painting, which evolved into a stencil design business in 1990. Donna also designs and hooks her own rug patterns and sells many of the patterns to other rug hookers, as well as selling finished rugs. She is a frequent contributor to Rug Hooking magazine, and takes part in a variety of shows and exhibits. For more information about her rugs, contact Donna at her web site www.blueribbonrugs.com.

Shaker Diamonds Table Mat Geometric

BY KEITH KEMMER

I love the old primitive rugs and the beauty of their simple designs that show what was important in the maker's life. But most of all, I love the unexpected use of color and nothing typifies this more than the use of hit-and-miss wool. Nothing is as beautifully simple as Shaker design, so for this mat I combined two influences—simple design and interesting use of color. This design is based on an early Shaker attributed rug from American Hooked and Sewn Rugs: Folk Art Underfoot, *by Joel and Kate Kopp.*

Shaker Diamonds Table Mat, 30" x 12", various cuts of wool on linen. Designed and hooked by Keith Kemmer, Waterford, Michigan, 2005.

Early rug hookers used any and all materials at their disposal to create true works of art. Scraps of many fabrics were used to fill backgrounds as well as main motifs. Over the years, as we have had better access to wools for hooking, the use of hit-n-miss diminished. Yet, one of the best ways to make a rug look primitive is by mixing many wools into a motif or background. Recently, I was at a workshop with teacher Barbara Carroll where we were looking at some small, simple Edyth O'Neill patterns. "What would you do with this pattern?" Barb asked. Her immediate response was to hook the motif in hit-n-miss. She was right.

The addition of color and texture will create a lot of interest in a simple motif. For a different example, take a look at one of Karen Kahle's (Primitive Spirit) rugs. Though not an immediate hit-n-miss, her technique is done by using many different colors to create a single color in a motif.

These techniques have been included in the *Shaker Diamonds* mat. We all have bags of wool strips that we keep around hoping they'll find a place in the next rug. Well, this mat will make a dent in using some of these orphan strips. In *Shaker Diamonds*, I have used the traditional hit-n-miss technique for the large center diamond. For the four smaller diamonds—many different reds, yellows, greens, and blues creates single-colored diamonds. The background and border use other techniques that are important in a primitive—directional hooking and odd spots of different wools.

Hooking Instructions:

Start by transferring the pattern to the backing. Make sure the outermost border is straight on the grain. The best way to do this is to use a pencil to measure the backing leaving 4" from the edges. and then draw the outer border with the pencil point. It will be easy to feel if you have crossed the threads of the backing by using a marker to darken this line. From here place the backing over the pattern, using a window or light table, or anything that will allow you to see the pattern through the backing. This is a primitive geometric so you do not need to be exact with the width and length of the border blocks. I actually prefer a design with some variance. If your border is a couple of rows different, don't worry. This is in con-

WHAT YOU NEED:

- **Backing material** of choice—I used linen— measured at 20" x 38" (the rug is 12" x 30"). This allows for 4" on all sides

- **Wool:** swatches measure approximately 4" x 18"

- **4 Small Diamonds:** 5 swatches each of 5 different reds, yellows, greens, and blues. Either as-is textures or overdyed

- **Large Diamond:** strips for the swatches listed above, plus lots of strips from prior rugs

- **Center Background:** $1/4$ yard + a swatch of a dark texture or antique black overdyed. Plus, 2 swatches of a gray or brown texture. Make sure they are different values from the main background wool.

- **Border:** 6 swatches of mid-to-dark neutrals— different from the three wools used in the center background.

- **$1/8$ yard of two different tans,** equal in value

- **End squares:** You should have enough left from the swatches used in the small diamonds to hook these, depending on how much you use in the large diamond.

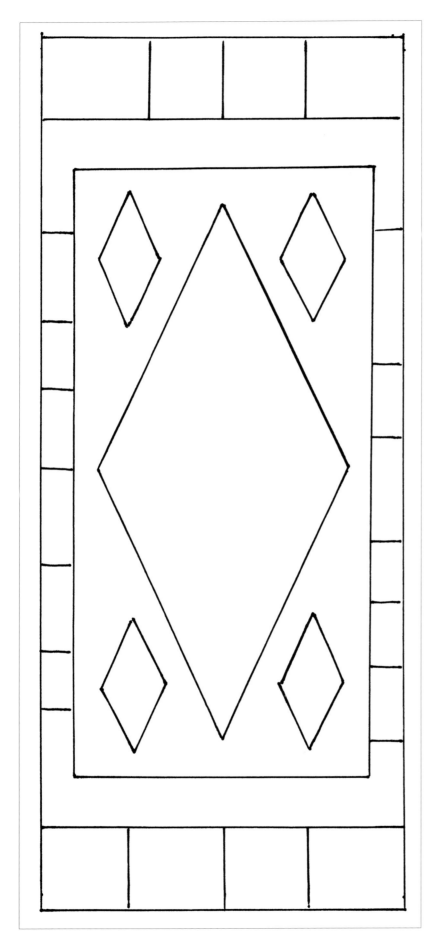

trast to a traditional geometric, which needs equal measure and spacing. However, I have retained some of the balanced structure of a traditional geometric. The diamonds are true diamonds—the end and side corners mirror each other. Feel free to hand draw these for an even stronger primitive look.

Start by hooking two rows of the background around the center diamond. Make sure to stay outside the diamond line. This holding line will let you see if the shape is pleasing and make it easier to fill using the hit-and-miss technique. Remember, you'll be filling with different colors, widths, and lengths; it would be easy to lose the shape without the holding rows.

Look at the main diamond motif and decide if you want to hook one side with dark values and the other light, as I've done. Or, another option is to go around the diamond using one color, then a different color for the next row as you work your way into the center. This will result in a great rug even if you don't feel comfortable with values. But, if the large diamond is hooked using the values, you may question if the value difference is strong enough. I did. Once the diamond was hooked and some of the background filled in, the values became more apparent. This is one of my tips for hooking—don't pull out hooking until the rug is complete. The values of a motif can and will change as the rug progresses. Watch what happens and learn from it.

With the hit-and-miss technique, you really need to have an idea of how to place the colors. It is random, but with some thought of playing colors off each other. You don't want large areas of one color; your eye should not stop at one spot. The best way to think about color placement is to use complementary colors next to, along side, or following each other. Complementary colors are: yellow and purple, orange and blue, red and green.

And they do what the name implies; they make each other "shine." But, they can also cancel each other—if you take equal amounts of true complements, they will visually go gray. I doubt you would have exact complements in equal amounts with your wools, but think about how one color will look next to another. It's okay to place a yellow beside a blue and red texture (blue and red make purple) for example.

Another way to vary the amount of a color is to use different cuts, or the number of loops hooked. I varied both of these in my large diamond. There are some colors that only have three or four loops, along with #12 cut strips next to #8s. I will use different cuts to fill a motif—even of the same wool. This helps create a primitive look, something unexpected.

Next outline the small diamonds with your background. Then fill each with one of the four basic colors—red, yellow, green, and blue. Each diamond will be a single color using many different wools in that color spectrum. These diamonds were hooked in rows, alternating textures and cuts for interest. I placed the direction of the rows in the red, green, and blue small diamonds to radiate out from the center diamond. The yellow diamond row direction parallels the center diamond. This was not originally intended, but I liked the unexpected direction and left it in—one of those "happy mistakes" that adds to the charm of primitive rugs.

Finish the center background using the three darks specified in the materials list. Small amounts of two different textures were used in "splotches." Many hookers prefer to randomly hook these alternate background wools in a "worm" pattern, filling with the main wool. This is fine. But I like to use them as different spots of background because I notice that a lot of the old rugs are done this way. It is personal preference.

For the border I continued with the use of neutrals, based off the center background, allowing the color in the diamonds to pop. The end border brackets are hooked using the two tan wools, each bracket being mainly hooked with one of the tans. I hooked

Designer's Tips:

1. Let your rug evolve. Have an idea what you want to do, but allow for inspiration to work its magic as you hook.

2. Build a wool stash. There is no such thing as too much wool. Buy $1/4$–$1/2$ yards of many different types of wool rather than a couple yards of one kind of wool. The exception is wool specifically for overdyeing with many colors.

3. Don't pull out wool until the rug is completely done. Colors and values change as the rug is hooked.

4. Experiment and learn. Analyze what you like as you are hooking, as well as on yours and others completed rugs.

5. Dye wool without a specific use—to become part of your wool stash. There is nothing better than pulling out overdyed wool that is perfect for your needs.

6. Hook what and how you like. Strive for good technique but do what works for you. Enjoy your hooking along with the finished rugs.

small sections with the alternate tan to marry the motifs. I also hooked a few rows here and there using colors from the center diamond. If you choose to do this, the color doesn't matter as much as the value. Just make sure the values are similar to the tans. You don't want these spots to jump. You'll be surprised with what you can get away with.

The six side border rectangles are hooked using six neutral wools ranging from lighter than the center background to a little darker. I intended these rectangles to look like I ran out of the background and decided to make a border. They create subtle interest and move your eye around the rug. These rectangles are hooked using random color sequence on each side. The only planning was to place a light next to a dark value to separate the rectangles.

For the ends of the rug I brought back the red, yellow, green, and blue from the small diamonds. The idea was to have it look like I had more backing to fill or the size of the finished rug was lengthened as the hooking progressed. Again, this was something unexpected and evolved as it was hooked. Another enhancement to the primitive look I was going for.

I hooked each of these squares in the same color sequence on each end (unlike

> ## *By holding it [the rug] up in front of a mirror and looking at it from across the room—the mirror flips the image. It's the same rug but different, and a good way to find out if something is working.*

the rectangle on the sides). The end squares of red and blue are hooked concentrically around the square, whereas the yellow and green squares are hooked basically in rows. But, I changed the direction of one of the yellow squares rather than switch color sequence. Also, with the yellow and green squares, I did go around the corners with a strip of wool if it was long enough to make a nice corner. I felt there was nothing wrong doing this since the rug is a primitive.

Once finished with the hooking it came time to do the binding, and there are many options. The first step is to steam the rug using a damp towel and iron, and then allowing time for the rug to dry. (Your steamed rug may feel slightly damp, but should never feel wet). My binding technique follows the instructions given in Barbara Carroll's book *The Secret of Primitive Hooked Rugs*. I found this technique gives the best finish, squarest corners, and, most importantly, the fastest way to do the binding.

To recap, I wanted some unexpected use of color, design, and hooking in my piece. It was planned, but it also evolved (another of my tips). When I started the rug I knew the center diamond was going to be hit-and-miss. I also thought the

small diamonds would be individual colors, but using a different hit-and-miss technique. Then in order to "pop" the colors of the diamonds a neutral background was planned. I decided to make it dark, since dark backgrounds tend to give colors a rich, jewel-like quality—and these are diamonds, after all. (Light backgrounds move colors toward bold and bright.)

Where the rug really evolved was the border. The biggest challenge was pulling in some of the color without conflicting with the diamonds. As the rug came together it "spoke" to me. I take many different wools and place them alongside the hooking, then I'll look at the rug from a different perspective, i.e. across the room, or in different light. Recently, while at a workshop I learned a new technique to get a different look at a rug. By holding it up in front of a mirror and looking at it from across the room—the mirror flips the image. It's the same rug but different, and a good way to find out if something is working. I was pleasantly surprised; hopefully you will be, too.

Any way you decide to hook your primitive—if you think it works—works! Just focus on making the best rug you can, utilizing good materials, and good hooking techniques, and you can't go wrong. ●

ARTIST: KEITH KEMMER

Being raised on goat's milk and lamb chops gave Keith an early affection for wool. Starting back in the '70s, he experimented with fiber, like a lot of us. The '80s gave way to art school and a short foray into black and white minimalism. Keith found his way back to fiber in 1989 as a weaver. With a focus on functional fiber, Keith weaves blankets, coverlets, towels (one of his Shaker reproduction towels is in the collection at The Shaker Village of Pleasant Hill), scarves, and rugs. In 1995, he mocked a flyer for rug hooking classes but soon found himself a "permanent student."
Keith's focus on hooking is with primitives, trying more and more to hook and design like the early
rug makers. He looks for beauty in the simple and the honest. "The early rugs have a timelessness and humility that comes
from the hooker's heart. It doesn't get any better than that!"

Harebells

BY KATHY MORTON OF MORTON HOUSE PRIMITIVES

Many of my beginning students are looking for new ways to finish off their smaller projects. Since my rug hooking classes are held in a quilt shop, we are inspired by many of the samples seen around the shop.

One of the owners of the quilt shop where I work is always on the look out for antique frames. She has collected many and stored them to frame all types of handwork.

Harebells, 10" x 12", #6- and 8-cut wool on monk's cloth. Designed and hooked by Kathy Morton, Eden Prairie, Minnesota, 2005.

WHAT YOU NEED:

Wool Requirements:

- 3"x 16" strip - #6 cut Texture it blue with green (Outline flower and detail lines)

- 5" x 16" strip - #8 cut Herringbone medium Yellow green (Flower stem)

- 1" x 16" strip - #8 cut Medium Gold - (Flower center)

- 3" x16" strip - #8 cut Gold green (Flower calyxes)

- 14" x 16" strip - #8 cut Two mixed medium blues (Front portion of petals)

- 4" x 16" strip - #8 cut Bright blue (Bud, flower inside, back two)

Petals:

- 20" x16" strip - #8 cut Two mixed taupes (Background)

- 5" x16" strip - #8 cut Dark taupe (Background squiggles)

- 2/3-yard fabric for making a border around hooking

One of my patterns, *Kate's Flag*, was being offered as a class. Because the size is rather diminutive, my boss took the piece and mounted it on a piece of foam core (found in fabric or art stores), and covered it with a coordinating cotton fabric. She hung the covered piece in one of her antique frames. I was immediately attracted to the look because it was a very simple way to enhance the hooking and have it displayed in an artistic way.

Since then, I have used this technique with cotton or wool to add a mat that adds size to my hooking piece as well as embellishing with coordinating colors.

To find a piece of fabric that goes well with your hooking requires taking the completed piece to a fabric store of choice. Try to check colors in the daylight to avoid a false sense of matching. If you have trouble with colors, ask for a clerk's help. This is especially true in a quilt store where they deal with color decisions every day.

Harebells Pattern

When I was teaching a workshop in Wisconsin, I stayed with a rug hooker who was also a master gardener. I love flowers and am especially drawn to those that have interesting shapes and colors in their blooms. When I got home I decided to do a Master Gardener Series that featured some of my favorite flowers based on color. *Harebells* was one of the first designed. Since blue is one of my favorite hues, and I have a couple types of bluebells in my garden, this was an obvious choice. The wool I chose was mainly as-is. I normally don't do that but seemed to be able to find the envisioned colors in my stash. I also planned on making up some kits for beginning classes and that was a good incentive for wool off the bolt.

Hooking

1. Hook the light blue outline around the flowers, not the bud.
2. Hook the gold center on the flower on the right.

3. Hook the calyxes on the flowers and bud.
4. Hook the medium blues for the main body of the flowers. Mix as you hook.
5. Hook the bright blue on the inside of the flower on the right, the two tips of the left flower, and the bud.
6. Hook the stem.
7. Hook the darker squiggles in the background. (I drew mine in free hand.)
8. Mix the medium taupes for the background. Hook two rows around the motifs.
9. At this point, sew on the fabric borders either by machine or hand. Measure the two sides of the hooking and pick the common number of inches. Cut two borders from the fabric that is 3" wide by the number determined above plus 1/2"(to facilitate a 1/4" seam allowance.) Sew this on and lightly press if needed. Watch the grain of the fabric if you are using a stripe or plaid. If you want a very primitive look, cut the fabric slightly off grain. Measure the top and bottom edges of the hooking plus the sewn-on borders. Again find one number and add for seam allowances. Sew these to complete the borders around the hooking.
10. Once your borders are sewn on, continue to hook next to the borders with two rows of straight hooking.
11. Finish the hooking of the background using swirls, etc, that echo the squiggle lines already hooked.
12. Block the hooked piece.
13. Purchase a piece of foam core that will fit inside your frame. If the finished piece is a fairly average size like 8"x 10" or 10" x 12", you could buy a frame in a store that isn't antique. Sometimes I will design a hooked pattern just to fit a particular frame that I already own.
14. Stretch the piece over the foam core. I use dental floss with a needle and stitch opposite sides of the piece to get an even distribution of pressure on the hooking. It is helpful to have an extra pair of hands when doing this. I also know people that have

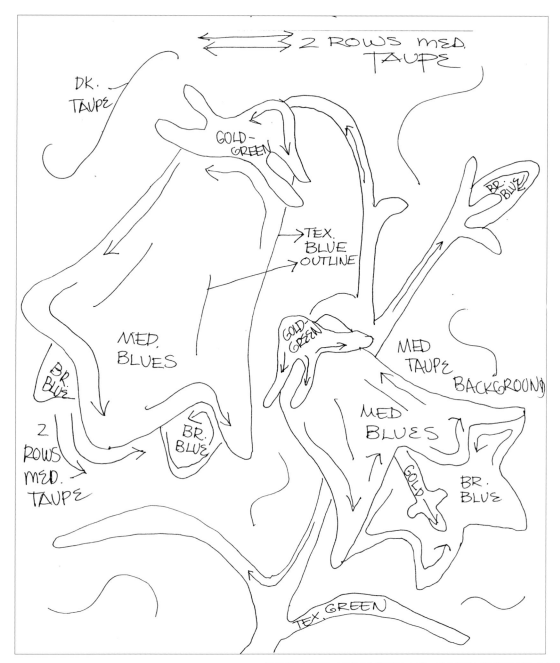

just used tape or a glue gun to attach the hooked piece to the foam core.

15. Keep watching how the hooking is centered on the foam so it is not crooked. When it is the way you want it, place in the frame. Tape it in with duct tape or use tiny brads, if the frame is very durable. If you buy a frame, it probably already has ways to hold in the framed piece.

16. I cover the hooking on the back with brown craft paper. If you spritz it with water, it will shrink and be very tight. The paper should be glued to the frame.

Designer's Tip:

If you are one of those hookers that works without aid of a teacher or who feels that color is not their thing, ***use the following process in reverse***. Go to your favorite fabric store and buy ¹/₃ or ¹/₂ of a yard of fabric that you truly love. I prefer a fabric that is not solid unless you are working on a hooking pattern that is very contemporary or Amish in feel. I use either a floral, geometric, or small print design. Remember, the colors need to be ones that you absolutely adore! Use this fabric to help you color plan the rug pattern. You don't have to exactly match each color in your yardage, but the wool choices should blend with what you bought. When I am using wool instead of cotton for the mat, I look for stripes or plaids. Some Pendleton pieces look especially striking on a small hooked mat.

Harebells Color Guide

Part of the Master Gardner Series, Morton House Primitives

Width	Color	Placement	
#6	Textured Light Blue	Outline Flowers, Flower Detail Lines	
#8	Textured Green	Stem	
#8	Gold	Flower Center	
#8	Gold-green	Flower Calyxs	
#8	Two Mixed Medium Blues	Flowers	
#8	Bright Blue	Bud, Flower Inside, Back 2 Petals	
#8	Two Medium Taupes	Background	
#8	Dark Taupe	Background Squiggles	

17. The frame in this project was one that hung in my grandparents home in northwestern Minnesota. It has great sentimental value to me and I love the fact that I am able to use it to embellish one of my hooked pieces. I made a note on the craft paper backing to indicate the history of the hooking and the frame. Remember to date your finished piece. ●

ARTIST: KATHY MORTON

Kathy has always loved color and textiles, and she started her hooking career in the mid-eighties. Her undergraduate work was in art education with a specialty in oil painting. In graduate school she switched to textiles as her major area of study. Kathy started Morton House Primitives 20 years ago, which has grown to include a mail order catalog as well as classes in her home studio and in a quilt shop in the Minneapolis area. Kathy currently teaches high school art, and in the summers, she travels throughout the U.S. doing workshops at camps and other studios. The pattern **Harebells** *is available on monk's cloth for a cost of $18 or primitive linen at $23.50. Add $4 for shipping and handling. For more information contact Morton House Primitives, 9860 Crestwood Terrace, Eden Prairie, Minnesota 55347; telephone (952) 934-0966 or kathymullvain@aol.com.*

My Turn

BY WENDY MILLER OF THE RED SALTBOX™

While browsing through old magazines and books for decorating ideas for my home, I came across a darling photo of a little girl and a sunflower. She was on her tip-toes reaching up to smell the sunflower. I thought it would make a wonderful rug. So I went to my drawing table, stacked up some crows to smell a sunflower, and My Turn was created!

Transfering the Pattern

Enlarge *My Turn* 400% to 24" x 30". Tape the enlarged paper pattern onto a glass patio or coffee table and then lay your linen on top. Place a lamp or other light source underneath the table to provide light up through the glass, the paper pattern, and the linen foundation. Get your linen positioned very square with your pattern. Using a permanent marker, trace the lines of the border first, making sure to follow one thread and draw your lines on grain. Always draw straight lines on the grain of the linen. After you have drawn all the borderlines, now make sure you are still lined up with your pattern. Then trace the crows and sunflower onto the linen.

Hooking Instructions

My Turn sample rug was hooked with #8$^{1}/_{2}$-cut wool strips.

1. Hook the outlines of the crows and then fill them in with either black wool or a combination of antique black wools. I used several plaid wools that had been overdyed antique black. Using a mill-dyed black will make your crows stand out more and appear bolder; while using antique blacks will make your crows appear softer.

   NOTE: If you plan to use old buttons for your crow eyes, then hook over the entire area of each crow as if the eyes were not there. When you are all finished, sew on old buttons for your crow eyes right on top of the finished hooked loops.

2. Hook an outline of the center of the sunflower with one row of rusty red. Then hook inside the rusty red outline, filling in the center of the sunflower with the black/mustard hound's-tooth wool.

3. Now hook each individual sunflower petal alternating different mustard wools for each petal. I used oatmeal wool and several different plaids that I had overdyed in a nice primitive shade of mustard for my sunflower petals. By using several different mustard wools, this allowed me to separate each of the petals, without outlining each individual petal. If you would prefer to use one mus-

---

WHAT YOU NEED:

- Wool yardage amounts are based on 60" wide wool (extra wool needed should you hook high or tend to pack your loops)
- $^{5}/_{8}$ yard of 5 mustard wools (combined total yardage)
- $^{1}/_{4}$ yard rusty red wool
- $^{1}/_{3}$ yard of 3 green wools (combined total yardage)
- $^{3}/_{4}$ yard black/mustard hound's-tooth or similar wool
- $^{1}/_{3}$ yard antique black wool
- 1 yard of 3 light tan/beige wools (combined total yardage)
- 34" x 40" of primitive linen (or other rug foundation)
- Permanent marker
- $3^{1}/_{3}$ yards of rug binding tape
- Carpet thread to match binding tape
- General hand-sewing supplies

My Turn, 24" x 30", #8^1/$_2$-cut wool on linen. Designed and hooked by Wendy Miller, Miamisburg, Ohio, 2005.

Wool samples used to hook *My Turn*.

tard for all of the sunflower petals, just hook a narrow separating row between each of the petals with a brown or black wool. A black line separating the petals will be harsher than if you used a warmer brown to separate between each of the sunflower petals.

4. Using various green wools, hook the stem and leaves of the sunflower. I used two similar greens and also added one slightly darker green wool strip to each leaf to create veining.

5. Now using the various light background wools, outline the crows and the sunflower with one hooked row to "lock" their shape. Hook one row of light background along the outside rectangle perimeter of the background area, just inside the borderlines. Now start "echoing" the shape of the crows, sunflower, and outside background rectangle, until the entire background is filled. Keep alternating between the three light background wools when filling in your background.

NOTE: 'Echoing' is the process of continuing to follow the shape of the motifs of the rug, hooking row after row around all shapes, until the entire background area is filled. Continue hooking around the crows and sunflower, and at the same time, be echoing the rectangle perimeter background shape as well. Eventually, the rows that are echoing

the crows and sunflower will intersect with the rows of the background rectangle and you will fill in the entire background.

6. Hook all the border outlines with one row of mustard/black hound's-tooth wool. Then hook one row around the outside edge of the border of the rug. Also hook one row for the inner borderline, just outside the last row of the background. Continue the single hooked row of the inner border, all the way out until it intersects the outer borderline.

7. Inside each of the four square corners of the rug, hook one row of antique black wool to outline the square shape of each inside corner square. Now with one of the mustard wools, hook the rectangle coil in each of the four corners as indicated on the pattern. Fill in between the rows of mustard of the rectangle coil, with a row of antique black wool.

8. To fill in each side section of the border, I used four different wools— mustard, green, rusty red, and the black/mustard hound's-tooth. Starting on one end of a side border section, right next to a corner block, alternate hooking rows of mustard and the black/mustard hound's-tooth in between the rows of green and rusty red. On the sample rug, I hooked my colors in the following order:

One row of each, starting next to a corner block:
- Mustard
- Black/mustard hound's-tooth
- Green
- Black/mustard hound's-tooth
- Mustard
- Black/mustard hound's-tooth
- Rusty Red
- Black/mustard hound's-tooth

> *If you would prefer to use one mustard for all of the sunflower petals, just hook a narrow separating row between each of the petals with a brown or black wool.*

Then start with mustard again and
repeat over and over, until the side section of the border is filled. Refer to picture of sample rug for hooking order if

necessary. Do all four sides of the border
this way, until all four are filled in solid.

Another great border idea for this rug
would be to hook the four sides as hit-and-

> *Another great border idea for this rug would be to hook the four sides as hit-and-miss. Use up all those leftover strips lying around everywhere.*

miss. Use up all of those leftover strips lying around everywhere! This would give the rug a stunning and colorful border and bring even more colors into the rug. Don't be afraid to change your rug and hook it differently than the sample rug.

Pressing the Rug

Press the rug with lots of steam, using a damp cotton towel between the iron and your finished rug. Press the back of the rug, and then turn it over and press the front of the rug. Repeat if necessary. Remember to use lots of steam. If the rug has lost its shape during the hooking process, now is the time to tug it into a nice rectangle shape again. Lay the rug on a flat surface and let it dry overnight.

Binding and Labeling the Rug

Bind the rug with the technique of your choice. This rug was bound using black cotton rug tape. The excess foundation was serged off (or cut off and zigzagged with a sewing machine). The rug tape was hand-sewn very close to the last row of hooking. Then it was folded over to the backside of the rug, and hemmed down. Make sure to miter and sew the corners of the rug tape down neatly. Give the rug another quick

pressing with lots of steam after binding. Again, lay it on a flat surface and let it dry overnight.

Label your rug with your name and the date, and any other pertinent information. If you don't have a label, one can easily be made out of muslin and the information written on it with a fine point permanent marker. Hand-sew the label securely onto the back of the rug.

Adding Old Buttons

I love to use old buttons on my rugs. To me, a primitive crow just isn't a primitive crow without an old button for an eye! If you're using old buttons for your crow eyes, then hand sew them on securely with carpet thread on top of your hooked loops, after the rug is all finished and pressed. ●

Designer's Tip

When choosing several different similarly-valued wools to blend in together for your rug's background, always pick one wool that is slightly darker or lighter in value than the other background wools. This wool will become your 'movement' wool, and it will add visual interest to the rug's background. Hook the movement wool evenly throughout the background of the rug. Refer to the sample rug of *My Turn* and notice that I chose one slightly darker wool value as my movement wool.

ARTIST: WENDY MILLER

Wendy Miller has been rug hooking since 1999. She is the designer behind The Red Saltbox™, *a primitive rug hooking company, whose patterns are known for being folksy and whimsical. She hooks in primitive wide cuts and her rugs have an instant 'old age' appearance to them. She is known for her use of textured wools and primitive color palette. Wendy has won numerous awards for her rugs at Sauder Village, Heart of Primitive, A Celebration of Hand-Hooked Rugs XV, and Rhapsody in Rugs. Wendy teaches primitive rug hooking seminars at her Red Saltbox studio, which is located next door to her home, a red saltbox. For more information about her studio, seminars, wools, or rug pattern line, visit her website at www.theredsaltbox.com.*

Madi's Favorite

BY MARGO WHITE

The inspiration for Madi's Favorite comes from the style of a simple antique appliquéd quilt design. Many early rugs were inspired from quilt patterns. Whether it was a whole quilt that was hooked into a rug, or just parts of the quilt design, this was a simple way for the rug maker to come up with a pattern.

I chose to make this rug a square design in order to keep the "feel" of a quilt. Many color choices would work well in this pattern and there is no reason to limit the color choices to only four, as I did here. However I feel that using only a few colors gives this rug an earlier look.

Preparing to Hook

First, decide what foundation you want to use: burlap, linen, or monk's cloth (which is what I used). Beginners find it easier to hook on monk's cloth, as it is "kinder" to your hands. Monk's cloth has a softer feel, and it is, therefore, easier to pull the wider, primitive, wool strips through the foundation fabric. Monk's cloth can stretch when pulled too tightly onto a hooking frame (as with other foundations). Place the foundation's grain straight on the frame and stretch gently and evenly along all sides. Never leave the pattern stretched on a hooking frame for long periods of time. Get in the practice of releasing the tension of the pattern when you are finished hooking for the day. This gives the foundation time to "relax."

The foundation needs to be about 8" larger than the finished pattern. This pattern measures 30" x 30", so the foundation needs to be at least 38" x 38". To prevent fraying, serge the edges, or sew a double row of zigzag stitching around the edge, or fold masking tape over the raw edge. When cutting the foundation, be sure to "pull" a thread and then cut in that space to insure that your foundation is "square."

When drawing or tracing the pattern, be sure to draw the outside edge of the pattern and the 1" border straight on the grain of the foundation. This is easily accomplished by using a pencil to draw this line in the "ditch" of the foundation. Once you have done that, you can take your black permanent fine-tipped marker and follow this pencil line. I use fine

WHAT YOU NEED:

- **Foundation:** At least 38" x 38"

- **Rug Binding Tape:** Black, $1^1/4$" wide

NOTE: Wool amounts are estimates, depending on cut of wool and your own hooking style.

- **Greens:** $3/4$ yard of assorted greens. Cushing dyes, Silver Gray Green, Khaki Drab, Khaki, Olive Green, and Bronze Green over any color of wool.

- **Tans:** $1/2$ yard of assorted tans. Cushing dyes $1/4$ teaspoon Medium Brown and $1/4$ teaspoon. Ecru over off white, oatmeal and tan wool.

- **Reds:** $3/4$ yard of assorted reds. PRO Chem Brick over light grays, light plaids, tans, and oatmeal wool.

- **Blacks:** 2 yards of all "antique blacks." I dye antique blacks with PRO Chem #672 jet black and either #819 purple, #822 plum, #502 chocolate brown, or #366 red. In a large pot I will use 1 to 3 tablespoons of #672 jet black with 1 tablespoon (or more) of any of the above over any color wool texture. Also, PRO Chem #503 makes a great antique black. A good way to always have "antique blacks" is to have a container that you put all black scraps into; this can and should be anything "dark." Then, when getting ready to hook with "antique blacks," just pull wool from this and consider it all black. This is a great way to get that faded black look that early rugs have.

Madi's Favorite, 30" x 30", #8-cut wool on monk's cloth. Designed and hooked by Margo White, Indianapolis, Indiana, 2005.

> *Get in the practice of releasing the tension of the pattern when you are finished hooking for the day. This gives the foundation time to "relax."*

tipped black (only) Sharpies to draw my patterns because they do not bleed when wet. I share my home with several cats, and having washed many rugs and even unhooked monk's cloth, I have tested the color-fastness of Sharpies firsthand.

To transfer the pattern, you can use nylon window screening, nylon net, or Red Dot tracer (light weight non-iron on interfacing works the same as Red Dot). I like the window screening the best. Tape the window screening over the pattern, and

- Finishing the rug is a very important part of a hooked project! The way it is steamed and bound is an excellent way to add that "aged" look to your project. When you consider the time and effort that has gone into designing the pattern, choosing the colors, possibly dyeing the wools, and hooking a piece, the same consideration should be put into the finishing. When a master craftsman builds a fine piece of furniture, they would never think of not applying the finish with the same care as they took in building the piece of furniture. This is the same time and care that needs to be put into finishing your hooked rug.

- If you study older rugs, you will soon see that they are not finished with a whipped edge. A simple folding of the foundation to the back of the rug is how most older rugs were finished. This edge was then sewed down to the back of the rug. Many times a piece is found where the edges were folded to the back and the last few rows were hooked through both the pattern and the edge of the folded foundation. Of course, there were exceptions with all rugs, but whipping with yarn was rarely done.

with your marker trace all the lines onto the screening. Next, tape or pin this screening over the "squared" rug pattern and trace through the screening. By having the borderlines squared on the foundation it is now easy to place your pattern in the center of the rug. Your pattern will now be on the foundation! Another way that works well with this pattern, since it has large motifs, is to trace each motif onto Mylar (a plastic template material found in craft or quilt shops). Cut the motifs out, and then position them on the foundation and trace around them. (Running a pencil line down the center of the pattern both ways helps in this positioning.)

Wool & Colors

There are only four colors used in *Madi's Favorite*. I find that using fewer "different" colors makes for a simpler, more antiqued look to a rug. Don't worry about all the reds, greens, tans, or black matching each other. Try to think simple (like a pioneer!) and pretend that there are very few choices of scrap wools to hook in your rug. Remember, many early rugs were hooked with what was on hand, so colors sometimes were very few.

Overdyeing different wools (solids, checks, tweeds, plaids, etc.) in the same dye pot for each color gives the variations in the colors. Use two or more different dye pots of green (same for reds, tans, and blacks) and then use wools from each dye pot in the rug. Don't worry about the colors matching perfectly; choose some a bit lighter or darker in value and even slightly different shades. Once the wools are ready, cut some of each of the different colors and values. Now mix these together like you would toss a salad. Do not pick and choose a strip as you hook; rather, reach into the pile of greens and hook that strip. Hook shorter strips at times to give a more varied look to the color. It will not matter that the same piece of wool might have been used several times together. When looking at the rug from a distance, the colors will all mesh together as if they were one. In other words, do not think too hard about your choice! Remember, an antique rug just might have been hooked by candlelight, or a very low watt light bulb, and that the hooker probably could not see the exact color!

Steaming

One of the most important and often overlooked aspects of hooking is the steaming of your finished rug. Lay a heavy

Don't worry about the colors matching perfectly; choose some a bit lighter or darker in value and even slightly different shades.

terry cloth towel on the ironing board and place the rug on top of it. Don't worry if the edges of the rug hang over the ironing board—just shift it as needed. Use a lightweight cotton dishtowel about the weight of a handkerchief as your pressing cloth. I use cotton feed sack dishtowel. These can be found very inexpensively at most discount stores. Wet the thin towel and place it on the rug. The purpose of this thin wet cloth is to let the moisture from the cloth and the heat from the hot iron "shrink up" the loops and give it that "already walked on" appearance. With the iron on its hottest setting and the steam on, press the iron on the dishtowel, holding it to the count of 10 before moving it to the next spot. Do not slide the iron over the wet cloth as though you were ironing, but rather pick it up and set it back down. Use some pressure while steaming. (I have actually used too much pressure in the past and broken my ironing board!) This pressing procedure, known as blocking, really helps to mesh the loops together and takes away that just hooked look. I press my rugs on both the front and back, always making sure to

The important thing to remember, no matter how you finish your rugs, is to please finish the edges in some way, as that edge is one of the weakest parts of the rug.

keep the pressing cloth very wet. When you've finished pressing the rug, if you find places that still look uneven, wet the cloth and press those areas again. In steaming this way I can assure you that your rug will truly lay flat!

Binding your Rug

After steaming, cut the foundation around the rug so that it is 2" from the finished hooking. To make sure this is a straight cut, clip a thread at the 2" mark and pull the thread from the foundation and cut on this line. Trim off 1" of foundation at an angle at each corner. Fold these corners to the back of the rug and steam. Now fold down 1" of the foundation around the sides of the rug and steam. Finally fold the sides over again towards the back and steam. The corners are now mitered and the cut edges are folded under and protected on all sides. Place your rug right side up in a spot where it will not be walked on for at least 24 hours or until it is completely dry.

Make sure the edges are folded under so that it may dry flat.

When the rug is dry, stitch the edges of the foundation to the back of the rug by hand, using a heavy thread such as carpet or "craft" thread. Sew through the edge of the turned-under foundation and the underside of the rug. Place the rug binding tape over the folded foundation and whip-stitch one edge as close to the last row of hooking as possible. Then stitch the other edge of the binding down to the back of the rug. Since you have a 1" folded edge of foundation on the back of your rug, the $1^1/4$" rug binding tape will cover the exposed foundation.

As with all hooking, there are very few "rules" that must be followed in order to hook a rug. This is my way of finishing a rug and I have given reasons as to why I choose this way. The important thing to remember, no matter how you finish your rugs, is to please do so in some way, as that edge is one of the weakest parts of the rug. ●

ARTIST: MARGO WHITE

As a child, Margo White's outlets for creativity included all sorts of needlework, along with learning to sew and design her own clothes. However, when she discovered rug hooking she "felt she'd come home." Along with hooking she enjoys designing and stitching all kinds of projects using wool. For over 10 years she has exhibited her finished rugs at wholesale and retail folk art and trade shows. She shares her passion for rug hooking through her "Primitive Rug Hooking Retreat" held annually at the restored Shaker Village at Pleasant Hill, Kentucky. Pleasant Hill lends itself to the 'retreat' type of atmosphere that goes with the relaxed style of primitive rug hooking. Patterns are available at: Margo White, 1120 Newgate Circle, Indianapolis, IN 46231, Simplywurthmorenecessities.com, mwhiterug@aol.com.

RUG HOOKING *Terms*

1. Cut—referred to as #3-#10

Wool can be cut into many different widths that are referred to by a number. Mechanical cutters can be purchased with heads or cartridges that will strip the wool into the widths you would like. As you can see from the chart below, #3 cut is the narrowest cut. The narrower the cut, the more definition and detail you can achieve. Most primitive rugs are hooked in a #6-#10.

* The number of the "cut" is equal to the number divided by 32 in inches. The chart shows the sizes of the various cuts from 3 through 8.

3	=	$3/32$"
4	=	$4/32$" or $1/8$"
5	=	$5/32$"
6	=	$6/32$" or $3/16$"
7	=	$7/32$"
8	=	$8/32$" or $1/4$"

* There are sizes larger than 8. For example, 8.5, 9, 9.5, 10, and 12. These cut sizes do not correspond to the measurements shown above and vary by individual cutter manufacturers. Contact the individual cutter makers to find out what size blades they offer and what the corresponding name for them is.

2. Backing—the foundation of your project

Your choice of foundation is important for strength, stability, and longevity.

There are backings made specifically for rug hooking. You will have to order these backings from the artists listed in the resource section as rug backing is not available in major craft supply stores. There are several types available:

- Linen—a soft, even weave material made from flax. It is strong and easy to work with. This is a more expensive product.
- Burlap—an inexpensive, durable backing. Burlap is not as evenly woven as linen, but is still a good product.
- Monk's cloth—a cotton backing that is soft and durable.
- Rug warp—also cotton backing that is tightly woven and very good for using a narrow cut of wool.

3. "As is" wool vs. hand-dyed wool—descriptive terms.

Many of the projects in this book call for "as is" wool. This generally refers to an undyed wool that is cut directly from the bolt and washed in warm water and dried in a dryer. Hand-dyed or over-dyed wool is exactly that: wool taken off the bolt or woolen clothing ripped apart that has been dyed another color. "As is" wool is less expensive than hand-dyed wool. Both are of equal quality.

4. Textured Wool—a descriptive term

Textured wool describes any kind of plaid, check, herringbone, or tweed design. Primitive pieces utilize textured wool to achieve a softer, aged look. They give a dimension to a rug that solid, flat wool cannot. Textures can be used "as is" or can be dyed.

5. Steaming—a finishing term

When your hooking has been completed, the next step is to steam the rug. This step will also be described as pressing or blocking. Not all rug hookers choose to steam their rug. The result of steaming is a softer feeling rug. It seems to even out the loops. The steps are simple:

- Spread out your hooked piece on a flat surface with an old towel or blanket under it.
- Wet an old hand towel.
- Place the wet towel in the center of your rug and with an iron set to steam, gently press down on the rug.
- Start from the center and work out, wetting the towel as needed . Do not press hard or move the iron in circles.
- Once the whole rug has been steamed, allow it to dry completely.
- If your rug does not lay flat in some areas, steam it again. Some people steam the back and the front.

GENERAL RUG HOOKING *Instructions*

Basic instructions to help you transfer a pattern, finish a rug, and hook with strips of wool

Transferring a Pattern to Backing

Beginning rug hookers often have problems figuring out how to transfer a printed pattern (such as we supply with our Dear Beginning Rug Hooker stories) onto a rug backing (burlap, monk's cloth, etc.). There are several ways to go about it, but the first step in all cases is to decide how big you want your rug to be.

Once you've determined that, a pen, ruler, and a little arithmetic are needed for one transferring method. Draw a grid over the printed pattern. For a simple pattern the grid's squares can be large; for a complex one, make them small. Use the same number of squares to draw a grid on the rug backing. To achieve proper proportions, calculate the size of the squares. Say you want your rug to be a 40" square, and you've used 8 squares across the top of your printed pattern's grid. 40÷8=5, so that means your 8 squares on the backing should be 5" on each side. You also used 8 squares down the side of the pattern, so you'll also use eight, 5" squares along the side as well. This grid will allow you to draw fragments of the pattern in the correct spot and in the correct proportion.

Another method employs a copy machine and nylon veiling (available at fabric stores). After you've used the copier to enlarge the pattern to the desired size, tape the veiling over it and trace all the lines onto the veiling. (It helps to have a transparent ruler to get the lines perfectly straight.) Then tape the marked veiling onto the backing. Retrace the lines on the veiling with a felt-tip pen so they bleed through onto the backing.

An iron-on pattern pencil that makes an indelible blue line can also help you transfer. (The pencils are available through suppliers who advertise in Rug Hooking.) Tape tracing paper over the pattern. Using a light table or a sunny window, trace the design onto the tracing paper with an ordinary pencil; turn the tracing paper over and draw over the lines with the pattern pencil, making a mirror image of the design.

Set your iron on high (cotton setting) and allow it to heat up well. Place the tracing paper with the mirror image down on the backing. Holding the paper securely, iron slowly over the design. Press hard, and do not move the iron around the design. Lift and reposition carefully until you have pressed the entire design. Be patient to allow enough time for the lines to be transferred onto the backing. (The pencil lines turn blue as they transfer.)

To check if the pattern has transferred successfully, lift a corner of the paper carefully so that it doesn't move. When all the lines are clearly visible on the burlap, it is ready.

Finish Before You Start

Finishing the edges of hooked pieces is critically important to improve their durability, particularly for floor rugs. When walked on for a number of years, poorly finished edges crack and split, requiring reconstruction that may be unsightly.

Unfortunately, even some experienced rug hookers do not finish their edges well. A quick review of common finishing techniques will benefit even the most seasoned rug hookers and may keep beginners from forming bad habits.

Before you begin hooking a pattern, machine stitch two rows around the perimeter as a defense against fraying. Stitch the first row $^1/4$" beyond what will be the hooked portion, and the second row $^1/4$" beyond the first row ($^1/2$" beyond the hooked portion). Overstitch each row of straight stitches with a row of zigzag stitches as shown in **Figure 1**.

After hooking the entire rug, vacuum it lightly and check it for mistakes. Lay it on a sheet wrong-side up and cover it with a damp towel. Stamp press it lightly with a dry iron to flatten it; do not rub it as if ironing clothing. Rehook bulging or uneven areas before finishing the edges.

The finished edge should be as high as the hooking, so select cording accordingly. Use preshrunk, natural-fiber cording: clothesline, heavy twine, etc.

Fold the backing toward the backside of the rug, about $^1/2$" from the hooked portion. Insert the cording and baste it into place with thread as shown in **Figure 2**. When whipped with yarn, the cording preserves the edge of the rug by taking the pressure of footsteps.

Dye woolen yarn to match your border or to coordinate with your color plan. After the cording is in place, whip the yarn around it with a blunt needle. You will use about one foot of yarn for each inch of whipping.

To whip the edge, simply sew yarn around the cording that is already covered with backing. Whip right up to the edge of the hooked portion on the front, out the back of the rug, around the cording, and down into the front again.

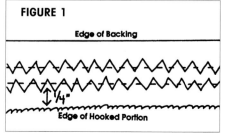

FIGURE 1

Edge of Backing

$^1/4$"

Edge of Hooked Portion

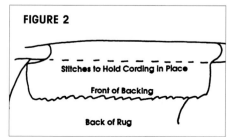

FIGURE 2

Stitches to Hold Cording in Place

Front of Backing

Back of Rug

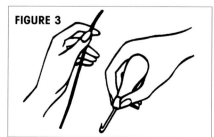

FIGURE 3

Continue around the perimeter of the rug, making sure the whipping covers the backing evenly. Do not start at a corner. At the corners, you will need to whip more stitches to cover the backing, and you will not be able to create perfectly square corners.

On the backside of the rug, handstitch 1¼" cotton binding tape right up to the edge of the whipping. Miter the tape and the backing at the corners. Cut away the excess backing so the raw edge is hidden under the tape. Finally, sew the inner edge of the tape between loops in the back of the hooked portion to cover the raw edge of the backing.

Sew a label onto the back of your rug. Include your name and location, the name and dimensions of the rug, the designer, the date, and any other pertinent information. Give the rug one final steam press as described above, using a much wetter towel. Lay it flat to dry.

How to Hook

These basic instructions apply to hooking with all widths of woolen strips. Step 3, however, applies to hooking with narrow strips in #3, 4, and 5 cuts. (The number refers to the numerical designation of a cutter wheel on a fabric cutting machine. A #3 wheel cuts a strip ³/₃₂" wide; a #5 cuts a strip ⁵/₃₂" wide; a #8, ⁸/₃₂" or ¼" wide, and so on.) Refer to the section on hooking with wide strips for special tips on holding a hook when making a wide-cut rug.

1 Stretch the backing in a hoop or frame with the design side up. Sitting comfortably, rest the hoop or frame on a table or your lap. The thumbscrew of a hoop should be opposite you.

2 With your left hand (right hand if you're a leftie) hold the end of a woolen strand between your thumb and forefinger (**Figure 3**).

3 With your right hand, hold the hook as if it were a pencil, with your fingertips on the metal collar as shown.

4 Hold the wool in your left hand and put it beneath the backing. With your right hand, push the hook down through the mesh. The shaft of the hook should touch your left forefinger and slide behind the woolen strip. Push the wool onto the barb with your left thumb.

5 With the hook, pull the end of the strip through to the front of the backing with the hook, to a height of about ½".

6 Push the hook down through the backing a little to the left of the strip's end and catch the strip underneath. Pull up a ⅛" loop, or as high as the strip is wide. To prevent pulling out the previous loop, lean the hook back toward the previous loop as you pull up another loop.

7 Working from right to left, make even loops that gently touch each other as in **Figure 4**. With fine strips, hook in almost every hole. Never put more than one loop in a hole.

8 When you reach the end of the woolen strip, pull the end up through the backing. Pull all ends through to the front as you hook. Tails on the back are untidy and can be easily pulled out.

9 Start the next strip in the same hole in which the last strip ended, again leaving a ½" tail.

10 Trim the ends even with the loops after making several loops with the new strip.

11 Continue the hooking process until the pattern is complete. To keep the back of the rug from becoming lumpy, do not cross a row of hooking with another strip. Cut the strip and start again.

12 Practice the following exercises to achieve the proper rhythm and technique: (a) after hooking straight lines, try wavy lines; (b) pack rows against one another to form a pile as in **Figure 5**.

Even the most skilled rug hooker must pull out loops now and then. Individual strands can be removed easily, but loops in packed areas are harder to remove. Use the hook or a pair of tweezers. Strands may be re-used if they are not badly frayed, and the blank area of the backing may be hooked again.

Hooking with Wide Strips

When hooking with wide strips (¼" to ½"), note that they pull up more easily if you hold the hook in the palm of your hand (**Figure 6**) and insert it into the backing at a sharper angle. (Some even prefer to hold the hook in this manner when working with narrow strips.) As with narrow strips, the shaft of the hook should rub the forefinger of your left hand and pass behind the woolen strip. The barb should hit your thumb, which pushes the wool onto the hook. Never loop the wool over the hook with your left hand; this will result in a lumpy back. If you cannot pick up the strip with your hook, the barb is not properly positioned.—*Happy and Steve DiFranza*

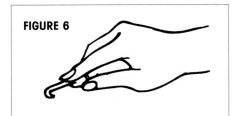

FIGURE 6

FIGURE 5

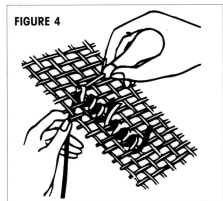

FIGURE 4

Finishing YOUR HOOKED PIECE

The following section outlines two of the most common ways of finishing your rug hooking projects. The first method is our favorite and the second method is an easy way to finish a hooked piece if you plan on attaching another edge.

METHOD 1: Whip Stitching to the Front

Our favorite finishing method for most of our projects is to wrap the linen to the front and whip with coordinating yarn. Detailed directions are below.

Supplies:
- Heavy-duty thread (quilting or upholstery)
- Embroidery needle
- Yarn for whipping (100% Wool)
- Large yarn needle
- Jute or other thin cord

1. Steam the finished piece using a wet towel. Steam the front of the piece and then flip it over and steam the back.
2. Zigzag around the piece close to the last row of hooking and again another inch away.
3. Trim close to the last row of stitching.
4. With right side up, fold the linen three or four times toward the top. Within the fold, insert one or two strands of jute. Hold in place and baste through the layers. I use quilting thread for this step. Upholstery thread or other heavy thread would also work well. (Basting may not seem necessary but it makes whipping go faster and it's a lot easier on your hands).
5. To turn the corners, trim the corners at an angle and fold in toward the hooking. Fold both sides in, forming a corner. Baste in place.
6. After you have basted around the piece, begin whipping. My favorite whipping yarn is worsted weight 100% wool yarn. You can dye the yarn to match. I use two strands of yarn to whip. Try using two colors or alternating colors. Have fun with this part! It can add a lot to your finished piece.
7. To begin and end each piece of yarn, do not tie a knot. Just weave the ends under the yarn that has been whipped.

METHOD 2: Twill Tape Binding

This is an easy method to finish rugs and is often seen on antique rugs. *It requires some preparation before hooking.*

Supplies:
- Sewing machine or needle and thread
- Cotton twill tape (washed, dried and pressed)
- Straight pins

1. Calculate the amount of tape you will need by measuring the perimeter of your rug and adding 3" **per yard**. The tape shrinks approximately 3" per yard when washed. Wash the tape in warm water and soap, rinse and dry. Press flat.
2. Lay your tape on the borderline of your design. The tape should be lying inside the design with its edge and the design's edge aligned. Pin in place. You may find it easier to sew around the corners if you finger press a mitered corner and pin it down. When you pin the beginning of the tape, turn the first inch towards you so that when all is done, there will not be a raw edge of tape exposed. When ending the length of tape, bring it over the folded edge and pin down. At this beginning/end, you will be sewing through three layers of tape.
3. Sew the tape around the border of the rug design, carefully easing your way around the corners.
4. When you pull back the tape, you should be able to see your design and the tape should extend into the selvedge about an inch. Baste the tape to the selvedge so that you will be able to hook right up to the seam.
5. Hook your design and steam it. Remove the basting and cut off the excess backing. Turn the tape under to the backside of your hooking and press it down. Blind stitch the tape to the underside of the rug, making sure to get your needle through the backing, not just wool loops. Sew the mitered corners down. When finished, steam the edges so all lays flat.

RUG HOOKING *Resources*

PATTERNS

Polka Dot Pillow
* *Katherine Porter*
  9985 Auburn Road
  Chardon, Ohio 44024
  (440) 286-4356
  fax (440) 286-1759
  loopdeeloorugs@yahoo.com

Table Scraps
* *Sally Kallin*, Pine Island Primitives
  16369 County 11 Boulevard
  Pine Island, Minnesota 55963
  (507) 356-2908
  rugs@pitel.net
  www.pineislandprimitives.com

Vanity Stool
* *Kim Nixon*, Under the Rug
  2117 Ludwick Drive
  Maryville, Tennessee 37803
  (865) 681-8733
  k_Nixon@bellsouth.net

Miss Liberty Hooked Rug
* *Beverly Goodrich*
  1404 Lakeshore Circle
  Gainesville, Georgia 30501
  (770) 287-8617

Handbag Slip Cover
* *Cindi Gay*
  315 Main Street, P.O. Box 83,
  Pemberville, Ohio 43450
  (419) 287-3884
  www.cindigay.com

Big Fish
* *Gail Dufresne*, Goat Hill Designs
  247 Goat Hill Road
  Lambertville, New Jersey 08530
  (609) 397-4885
  GailDuf@aol.com
  www.goathilldesigns.com

Gram's Pocket Purse
* *Kim Dubay*, Primitive Pastimes
  410 Walnut Hill Road
  North Yarmouth, Maine 04097
  (207) 829-3725
  KimDubay410@aol.com

Geometric Pillow
* *Sally Korte & Alice Strebel*
  Kindred Spirits, 115 Colonial Lane,
  Kettering, Ohio 45429
  (937) 435-7758
  www.kindredspiritsdesigns.com

Log Cabin Collection
* *Susan Feller*, Ruckman Mill Farm
  P.O. Box 409
  Augusta, West Virginia 26704
  (304) 496-8073
  www.ruckmanmillfarm.com

Fantasy Garden Tote
* *Susan Quicksall*, Holly Hill Designs
  3420 County Road 315
  Oglesby, Texas 76561
  (254) 470-2014
  deqslq@aol.com

A Slice of Summer
* *Jenny Rupp & Lisa Yeago*
  The Potted Pear
  7045 Pinemill Drive
  West Chester, Ohio 45069
  (513) 759-5301
  thepottedpear@fuse.net

Funky Hooked Belts
* *Katie Fishbune*
  1309 Fox Glen Drive
  St. Charles, Illinois 60174
  (630) 513-0525

Rose and Bud Eyeglass Case
* *Karen Kahle*, Primitive Spirit
  P.O. Box 1363
  Eugene, Oregon 97440
  (541) 344-4316
  www.primitivespiritrugs.com

Old Saint Nick
* *Kris Miller*, Spruce Ridge Studios
  1786 Eager Road
  Howell, Michigan 48855
  (517) 546-7732
  www.spruceridgestudios.com

Hospitalitea Tea Cozy
* *Donna Hrkman*, Blue Ribbon Rugs
  3451 Wellington Drive
  Dayton, Ohio 45410
  (937) 254-2319
  donna@blueribbonrugs.com

Shaker Diamonds Table Mat Geometric
* *Keith Kemmer*
  4001 Saginaw Trail
  Waterford, Michigan 48239
  (248) 674-7087

Harebells
* *Kathy Morton*
  Morton House Primitives
  9860 Crestwood Terrace
  Eden Prairie, Minnesota 55347
  (952) 934-0966
  kathymullvain@aol.com

My Turn
* *Wendy Miller*, The Red Saltbox
  7757 Upper Miamisburg Road
  Miamisburg, Ohio 45342
  (937) 847-2162
  www.theredsaltbox.com

Madi's Favorite
* *Margo White*
  1120 Newgate Circle
  Indianapolis, Indiana 46231
  (317) 839-8994
  www.simplywurthmorenecessities.com

COMPANIES

* Rug Hooking Magazine
  5067 Ritter Road
  Mechanicsburg, Pennsylvania 17055
  (717) 796-0411
  www.rughookingonline.com
  rughook@stackpolebooks.com

* American Folk Art & Craft Supply
  604B Bedford St. (Rt. 18)
  Abington, Massachusetts 02351
  (781) 871-7277
  www.americanfolkartonline.com
  Made to order custom braided rugs,
  rug hooking supplies, and penny rug
  supplies and classes.

* Black Sheep Wool Designs
  Rhonda and Marty Manley
  (816) 781-6844
  www.blacksheepwooldesigns.com
  Featuring a full line of rug hooking
  supplies, patterns, and wool.

* Bolivar Fabric Cutter
  P.O Box 539
  Bridgewater, Nova Scotia B4V 2X6
  (902) 543-7762
  www.BolivarCutter.com

* By the Door Hooked Rugs
  Deanne Fitzpatrick
  RR 5, 19 Pumping Street Road
  Amherst, Nova Scotia B4H 3Y3,
  (800) 328-7756
  www.hookingrugs.com
  Complete line of supplies, kits, and
  patterns.

* Dorr Mill Store
  P.O. Box 88,
  Guild, New Hampshire 03754
  (800) 846-3677
  dorrmillstore@sugar-river.net
  www.dorrmillstore.com
  Quality wools, color palettes,
  patterns, kits, and much more.

* Green Mountain Hooked Rugs
  Stephanie Ashworth Krauss
  146 Main Street
  Montpelier, Vermont 05602
  (802) 223-1333
  *www.GreenMountainHooked
  Rugs.com*
  Patterns, supplies, and the annual
  Green Mountain Rug School.

* Halcyon Yarn
  12 School Street
  Bath, Maine 04530
  (800) 341-0282
  www.halcyonyarn.com
  service@halcyonyarn.com
  High-quality rug yarn for finishing
  hooked rugs.

* Harry M. Fraser Company
  433 Duggins Road
  Stoneville, North Carolina 27048
  (336) 573-9830
  fraserrugs@aol.com
  www.fraserrugs.com

Cloth-slitting machines, hooking,
and braiding supplies.

* Hartman's Hook
  Cindy Hartman
  P.O. Box 6536
  Williamsburg, Virginia 23188
  (33) 603-0057
  hhooks@mac.com
  www.HartmansHook.com

* Jane Olson Rug Studio
  P.O. Box 351
  Hawthorne, California 90250
  (310) 643-5902
  (310) 643-7367 (fax)
  www.janeolsonrugstudio.com
  The total rug hooking and braiding
  supplier for 33 years.

* Meno Trigger Grip
  983 Union Lane
  Little Suamico, Wisconsin 54141
  (920) 826-2880
  meno@new.rr.com
  www.menotriggergrip.com

* PRO Chemical & Dye
  P.O. Box 14
  Somerset, Massachusetts 02726
  (800) 228-9393
  (508) 676-3908 (fax)
  www.prochemical.com
  Dyeing supplies.

* Rigby Cutters
  P.O. Box 158
  249 Portland Road
  Bridgeton, Maine 04009
  (207) 647-5679
  Cloth stripping machines.

* The Wool Studio
  706 Brownsville Road
  Sinking Spring, Pennsylvania 19608
  (610) 678-5448
  rebecca@thewoolstudio.com
  www.thewoolstudio.com
  Quality woolens, specializing in
  textures for the primitive rug hooker.
  Send $5 for swatches.

* Wooley Fox, LLC
  Barbara Carroll
  132 Woolley Fox Lane
  Ligonier, Pennsylvania 15658
  (724) 238-3004
  www.woolleyfox.com
  Primitive patterns, custom kits,
  Gingher scissors, and other supplies.

* Woolrich Woolen Mill
  Catalog Orders
  Two Mill Street
  Woolrich, Pennsylvania 17779
  (570) 769-6464
  (Ask for Mill Sales, ext. 327)
  rughooking@woolrich.com
  Factory direct rug hooking wool.

ABOUT THE *Magazine*

Our Beginnings

In the 150 years since rug hooking made its way to North America, no periodicals covered the subject until professional rug designer Joan Moshimer began publishing *Rug Hooker News & Views* in 1972, a newsletter "by and for rug hookers." But as more people took up the craft and the rug hooking industry flourished, it became apparent that only a full-fledged magazine could best serve the growing audience.

In 1989, Stackpole Inc., a Pennsylvania-based book and magazine publisher, transformed Joan's newsletter into *Rug Hooking,* the only full-color, internationally read magazine devoted exclusively to the subject of hand-hooked rugs.

An Inside Look at *Rug Hooking* Magazine

Rug Hooking brings its readers striking color photographs of gorgeous rugs and stories that both inspire and instruct. Each issue of *Rug Hooking* contains articles on dyeing, color planning, designing, hooking techniques, rug hooking history, and more. Feature articles cover topics ranging from elaborate Orientals to country-style primitives.

The magazine's departments include **Dear Beginning Rug Hooker,** which presents a step-by-step project from a leading designer. Readers can follow the lesson plan, then hook their own rug using the *free pattern* included in the issue. **Colors to Dye For,** contains dyeing tips and formulas. **Reader's Gallery** exhibits one accomplished rug hooker's body of work. **Teacher Feature** lets readers in on a noted teacher's classroom lessons. **Elements** focuses on a specific design element or technique. **Beyond Our Borders** introduces rug hookers to other fiber arts, such as braiding and appliqué, which can be used to enhance hooked pieces.

Issues of *Rug Hooking* also contain **Date Book,** an engagement calendar listing events, classes, and gatherings; **Camps & Workshops,** profiling a rug school; and **The Loop,** linking rug hookers with each other.

Books From *Rug Hooking*

In addition to publishing five issues of the magazine each year, *Rug Hooking* also publishes books, of which **Celebration of Hand-Hooked Rugs** is one. Through the years *Celebration* has brought hundreds of beautiful rugs to the attention of rug hookers worldwide.

The Framework Series was introduced in 1998 with the publication of **People and Places: Roslyn Logsdon's Imagery in Fiber; Recipes From the Dye Kitchen;** and **The Pictorial Rug.** Other books include **Preserving the Past in Primitive Rugs** by designer Barbara Brown; **A Rug Hooker's Garden,** in which 10 experts teach how to hook a bouquet of blossoms; **The Complete Natural Dyeing Guide** by Marie Sugar, offers 89 natural dye recipes with natural ingredients; **Hooking with Yarn** by Judy Taylor; **Hooked on the Wild Side** by Elizabeth Black, a recognized expert on hooking animals, both domestic and wild; **Mary Anne Lincoln's Comprehensive Dyeing Guide** by Mary Anne Lincoln, a compilation of 10 years of articles in her magazine column; **The Rug Hooker's Bible** by Jane Olson and Gene Shepherd, based on 30 years of **The Rugger's Roundtable** newsletter.

Our most recent books include **Basic Rug Hooking,** a compilation of 12 beginner's projects and directions on design, color planning, wool selection, and hooking techniques, plus exclusive pull-out patterns; **The Secrets of Finishing Hooked Rugs** by Margaret Siano, which offers complete directions for each finishing technique; **The Secrets of Primitive Hooked Rugs** by Barbara Carroll, who takes you step-by-step through the process of creating a full-size Wooly Horse pattern; **The Secrets of Color in Hand-Hooked Rugs** by Betty Krull, an expert on color-planning and color theory; and **The Secrets of Planning and Designing Hand-Hooked Rugs** by Deanne Fitzpatrick, a well-known Canadian author on rug hooking and a member of our Editorial Board.

Books and magazines aren't the only way we communicate with the rug hooking community. Our *web site* (www.rughookingonline.com) is packed with vivid photos, informative text, and links to other helpful sites.

Rug Hooking's objective is to be the primary source of information and inspiration for rug hookers of all levels of experience. Since 1989 we have met that objective, and we intend to continue to do so for all the diverse and talented rug hookers found throughout the world. ■

For more information on Rug Hooking *magazine and its other publications, write to 5067 Ritter Road, Mechanicsburg, PA 17055 or call (800) 732-3669.*